Writer/Director
Amy Carroll
Art Direction
Debra Lee

Photography
Jan Baldwin
Wardrobe & Props
Tamsin Summers
Continuity
Debra Grayson

ACKNOWLEDGMENTS

Dorling Kindersley Ltd. would like to thank all those listed below for their help:

THE CAST

Rick Morris (Inspector Black)

Hassan Amini, Chris Arch, Chris Baldwin, Jan Baldwin, Joe Baldwin, Debra Blades, Ngaio Bowthorpe, Paul Bowthorpe, Denise Brown, Pete Caines, Louise Caldwell, Amy Carroll, Matthew Carroll, Zoe Carroll, Paul Checkley, Chinna the dog, Christopher Fouracre, Kate Holmes, Adrian Horne, Louise Howard, Paul Jones, Rex Lombard, David MacDougall, John Macintosh, Patrick Makin, Fred May, Derrick McClintock, Mark Melton, Kumars Mogtader, Rick Morris, Daniel Q. Naiman, Paul Nelson, Dean Nobes, Pheros Nosher, Cedric Paine, Suzie Pote, Kate Potter, Mary Priefert, Humphrey Price, Corinna Pyke, Caroline Robinson, Frankie Rossi, Marie-Therese Rossi, Luke Schiller, Sebastian Scott, Adrian Sharpe,

Ben Summers, Martin Summers, Tamsin Summers, David Taubman, Paul Treasure, Simon Turnbull, Justin van Soest, Marion van Soest, Henry Wynn, Adrian Yarme.

Props

Peter Cooling, Dr. & Mrs. E.D. Forster and Mr. & Mrs. R. Summers

Locations

Amy Carroll, Tessa Jones, Tony Papaloizou and Clare Spencer

Illustrator

Sean MacGarry

Retoucher

Nick Oxtoby

Photographic Services
Welbeck Photoprinters

Typesetting
Rowland Phototypesetting (London) Ltd

Reproduction
Repro Llovet, Barcelona

Many thanks to the following for their technical help: Chris Barnet, Peter Durant at LRT, Trevor Johnson and Melanie Miller

Library of Congress Cataloging in Publication Data
(Revised for volume 3)
Main entry under title:
Scotland Yard photo crimes from the files of Inspector Black.

Cover and spine title:
20 solve them yourself photo crimes.
Vol. 3 has title: Photo crimes.
"A Fireside book" — V. 3.
1. Puzzles. 2. Detective and mystery stories.
I. Black, Henry, 1890-1963. II. Title: 20 solve them yourself photocrimes. III. Title: Photocrimes.

GV1507. D4536 1983   793.73   83-11084
ISBN 0-671-47303-4 (v. 1)
ISBN 0-671-60568-2 (v. 2)
ISBN 0-671-62756-2 (v. 3)

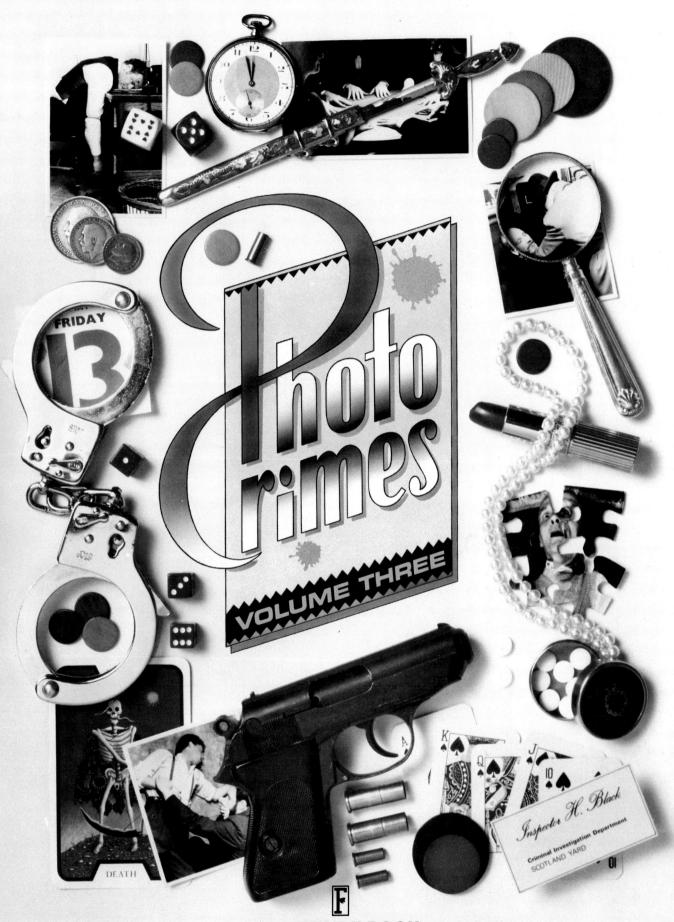

Photo Crimes

VOLUME THREE

A FIRESIDE BOOK
PUBLISHED BY SIMON & SCHUSTER, INC · NEW YORK

Dear Reader,

This being the third volume of *Photo Crimes*, you may already be acquainted with Inspector Henry Black and his cases. You will, no doubt, have been eagerly awaiting this further selection. However, should it chance that the other volumes eluded your grasp, you will find out all you need to know about my illustrious relative below.

Inspector Henry Black (1890-1963) was one of Scotland Yard's finest detectives, and my great-uncle. He was among those few who were responsible for refining the techniques of criminal investigation and, in part, creating the modern detective. Evidence was all that mattered to him and he believed that only education and experience could make a good detective.

Great-uncle Henry was a passionate communicator and copious note-taker. He was always ready to pass on his expertise in crime solving to his contemporaries and even to myself, his much-admiring great-niece. Long before he retired from the force, but after he was taken off active duty, he used to instruct younger colleagues on the finer points of detection with reference to his "master" cases. These consisted of a range of incidents – murders, kidnappings, thefts, suicides, extortions – which had occurred during the height of his investigatory career in the 1930s. Each case was a testimony to his genius as a crime solver.

He used to present these cases in the form of a slide show accompanied by notes of how he had proceeded. His students were then required to identify the culprits and give their explanations of how the deeds were accomplished. If the class had trouble reaching the correct solution, they could refer to certain clues and the suspect's statements. Great-uncle Henry's cases were extremely popular, but when he retired, so did his file. It was packed away in the attic along with his other memorabilia after his death.

And there it might have stayed were it not for a chance conversation at a crime writer's convention. A member of the association, and a chief inspector at Scotland Yard, was bemoaning the lack of detecting talent among new recruits. "No one seems to know a good clue from a red herring anymore. Crime laboratories are fine," he went on, "but these chaps think it's all done there."

That set me thinking. Perhaps Great-uncle Henry's master cases needed to be recalled from oblivion. He'd made crime solving fun while at the same time instilling a healthy respect for evidence. Perhaps it was time that his detecting acumen reached a wider audience.

Photo Crimes, then, is my attempt to make Great-uncle Henry's file a test of detecting ability for today's reader. I've left the cases as he wrote them up, including some of his master observations, all relevant clues (and some red herrings just as he would have used), the suspects, and his descriptions of what actually did happen, but I've presented his slides as photographs. Great-uncle Henry's marking system also can be used to keep score and preserve the "game" quality of his cases. You win or lose points according to the time elapsed, number of clues referred to, whether you chose the right or wrong suspect, or the right suspect for the wrong reason, etc.

You'll find that Great-uncle Henry's cases will require concentration, keen powers of observation, and a good understanding of character as well as the ability to think things through.

As you go through the book, keep a record of your score for each case on your Master Record, see page 64. At the end you'll discover whether Great-uncle Henry would have thought you Scotland Yard material or not.

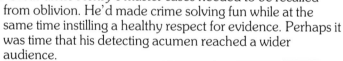

Good luck and good detecting !

HOW TO PLAY THE GAME

Have handy a pencil or pen and a piece of paper to make notes, your scorecard to record your points and penalties, and a clock or watch to record your time. Then:

1. Read each case through carefully, studying the pictures and captions.

2. If you haven't a clue as to how it was done or by whom, turn to one or more of the clues listed, but remember — they cost you points.

3. If you think you know who the culprit is, answer the questions on his or her suspect's "card". *Bear in mind that in "suicide" cases, the victim can also be questioned.*

4. Look up your answer on the evidence pages. If you've proved your detecting ability you will be awarded points and a chance to look at the truth: if your crime solving is not up to the mark, you will lose points and may be advised either to look at a clue or try another suspect.

5. When you've answered correctly and have read the truth, make sure you have entered the correct points and penalties on your scorecard. Then add your overall score to your Master Record under the appropriate case heading.

Was he likely to be on foot?

Yes **1**   No **2**

Would he prove to be above suspicion?

Yes **3**   No **4**

Ans. **H** ....

MR X

You must answer both questions, in which case your final answer will always consist of a letter and a number. In this example, if you think the answer to both questions is "Yes", you would write 13 on the answer line. When you refer to the evidence your answer will be under 13, line O.

HOW TO SCORE

Different points and penalties are awarded depending on the difficulty of the case, the time it takes you to reach the correct solution, the number of clues referred to, and how many suspects you have to question.

EASY	MEDIUM	DIFFICULT
The Riddle of the Sands	Torch Song Tragedy	Too Close a Shave
Fare to Nowhere	A Winter's Tale	The Taking of Little Zoë
Man's Worst Friend	Secrets of the Deep	Deadly Hobby
The Covent Garden Mob	Quarrel at the Quarry	Pembroke's Poser
Inside Job	Dressed to Kill	A Problem of Security
High Street Murder	Daring Death	Ill Met by Moonlight
Marital Mishap	Repairing Fences	

The Cases

Great-uncle Henry classified his cases as easy, medium and difficult. You will be awarded 100 points for the correct solution to an easy case, 150 points for a medium one and 200 for a difficult case. When you've chosen the right suspect and answered the questions correctly, you will find your winning score on the evidence page.

NB As a police cadet you are considered to have accumulated 50 points before you begin on your first case, The Riddle of the Sands. Make certain you add this to your score, but only once.

Time

Easy cases earn 20 points if done within 15-20 minutes, 10 points if done in 20-30 minutes but no bonus points if it takes you more than 30 minutes; medium cases earn 30 bonus points if done in 15-20 minutes, 20 points if done in 20-30 minutes and 10 points if over 30 minutes; difficult cases earn 40 bonus points if done in 15-20 minutes, 30 points if done in 20-30 minutes and 20 points if it takes you over 30 minutes.

Clues

Each clue costs you 10 points in a difficult case, 15 in a medium one and 20 in an easy case. Red herrings are the same in all, minus 20 points from your score.

Suspects

The questions accompanying the suspects are supposed to test your detecting ability. Therefore, all completely wrong answers cost you 30 points, but if you answer the questions correctly, even though the suspect is wrong or, if you chose the right suspect but answer the questions incorrectly, you will lose between 10 and 25 points. In the example on the right the player has questioned one wrong suspect (losing 25 points) before guessing the culprit (earning 150 points). He or she has referred to two clues (losing 30 points) and completed the puzzle in good time (earning 30 points). The player would thus have won 125 points for that puzzle.

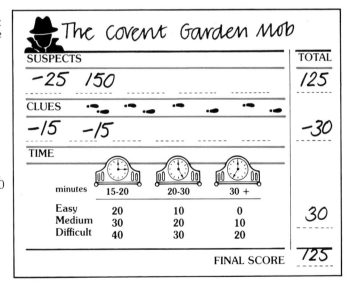

The Covent Garden Mob

SUSPECTS					TOTAL
−25 150					125
CLUES					
−15 −15					−30
TIME					

minutes	15-20	20-30	30 +	
Easy	20	10	0	30
Medium	30	20	10	
Difficult	40	30	20	

FINAL SCORE   125

MAKING A SCORE CARD

You will find it easier to determine your score if you use a card. You can duplicate the one shown here by tracing over it. Make certain, however, you leave out the filled-in information.

WHO CAN PLAY?

Photo Crimes can be worked singly, with a partner or against a competitor or competitors.

THE RIDDLE OF THE SANDS

It is not unusual for a person involved in a crime to eventually confess his or her guilt even when he or she has gotten away with it. It's not unusual, but . . . .

1 Inspector Black had had the unsolved murder of "Candles" Baker on his files for several months when new evidence seemed to implicate "Shorty" Reynolds.

2 Reynold's old girlfriend Barbara Tanner suddenly turned up to say she'd been with Reynolds when he shot Baker.

3 Not only that, but she'd stayed with him while he buried the gun near a beach hut in Hastings.

4 She was also able to point out the exact spot to Black, who after some digging produced the wicked looking weapon.

5 Sure enough, three of the cartridges were missing – Baker had been shot three times.

6, 7 "Do you mean to tell me you stood by while Shorty killed Baker and that only now, for some reason, you wanted to tell. Why you could be put in gaol as an accessory!"

"I have my reasons," growled Barbara, and except for some rather uncomplimentary personal remarks about Shorty, would say nothing else.

CANDLES BAKER

UNSOLVED

PENDING FURTHER INVESTIGATION

8 Black felt this latest development needed some looking into, so he paid a visit to Wormwood Scrubs. Shorty had been inside the last two months on a breaking and entering charge.

9 Told there was new evidence to connect him with Baker's killing, Shorty refused to change his original story.

10 "Like I told you guys, I spent the evening with my friend Gloria, and I've never been to Hastings in my life."

11 Gloria, Black remembered, claimed to have spent the entire night with Shorty playing gin rummy.

???

"This looks bad for Shorty," thought Black, **"but some further questioning should clear it up."** Whom did he have in mind?

Chance a clue? 8 33

Choose your suspect:
Gloria Harris, p. 56
Shorty Reynolds, p. 58
Barbara Tanner, p. 59

¿¿¿

FARE TO NOWHERE

Taxi drivers are supposed to be masters of the "knowledge," but was this one's incomplete?

1 Inspector Black looked inside the taxi, and at the man sitting upright in the centre of the back seat – a knife through his heart.

2 He looked inquiringly at Fred Rogers, the driver, who nervously fingered his cap.

3 "This bloke and his lady friend was standing in front of the Ritz Hotel when I dropped my other fare off.

4 "They got into the cab, and I had to drop her off near Sloane Square.

5 "She got out, leaned over this bloke. I thought she kissed him or something, then told me to drive him to an address in Kew.

6 "He wasn't a talkative bloke so I kept on driving – made every light – and got there in record time. However, he made no move to get out.

7 "That's when I turned around to have a close look at him. You could have knocked me over with a feather when I saw the knife in his chest. I felt his pulse, knew he was dead and hot-footed it back here.

8 "A cab seems a strange place to do yourself in – or maybe *she* did it when I wasn't looking."

9 Given Rogers' description, Black managed to track down Miss Polly Malone, who claimed her companion, Sir Lionel Livingstone, was perfectly all right, if a little drunk, when she had left him.

10 She admitted though that Sir Lionel was a bit of a raver, given to bragging about his money and his wild adventures. But she certainly had no reason to kill him. In fact, Sir Lionel had always been extremely generous to her....

11 Black, however, had already contacted the couple they'd had dinner with on the night in question, and they'd testified to a terrible row between the couple.

???

Black knew Polly Malone had lied to him, but did Rogers know more than he was saying?

Chance a clue? 2 27

Choose your suspect:
Polly Malone, p. 57
Fred Rogers, p. 58

MAN'S WORST FRIEND

One of the parties to this bizarre incident couldn't talk but his actions spoke volumes . . .

1 Inspector Black needed a strong stomach the day he'd been called to investigate the death of Barnabas Talgarth, a wealthy eccentric. The man lay out on his lawn, except for a horrible wound at his throat, his appearance was quite normal.

2 Phoebus, Talgarth's pet hound, sat dazed in the corner, restrained by a stout rope.

3 Talgarth's brother, Peter, was still shaken but able to tell Inspector Black what had happened. The two men normally worked from 10-11 in the garden Monday mornings. Barnabas would rake the leaves while Peter would take care of the shrubs.

4 That Monday, as usual, they'd tied the dog up in the house while they got on with their hour's work. Phoebus, who was rather bad-tempered, barked furiously and fought against the rope a great deal.

5 Suddenly, the dog managed to get loose and immediately attacked Peter. Barnabas rushed to his assistance and, though bitten, was able to get the dog off Peter.

6 However, Phoebus turned on Barnabas, grabbing him savagely by the neck. Peter was too weak to interfere and the dog's attack proved fatal.

7 Then, to Peter's horror, the dog once again turned on him. Though he defended himself with the secateurs he was only saved by the appearance of a quick-thinking milkman who managed to stun the dog with a stick.

8 The milkman, out on his normal rounds, had heard loud barking at about 10.45. He'd followed the sounds until he reached the Talgarth's garden. He'd been shocked to see Peter Talgarth grappling with his brother's pet dog. The dog was pretty excited so he'd hit him to separate them.

9 Inspector Black took a good look round the garden and noticed the rake and garden fork. Both looked relatively new. About a quarter of the small garden had been raked.

10 He walked over to Phoebus, who was quiet now, and except for a bump on the head, seemed in good shape.

11 Black rang Talgarth's solicitor who said his client was a wealthy man, of good health, but extremely frugal with his money. Peter Talgarth was his heir.

???

Inspector Black took another look at Phoebus. It was a shame to put down such a fine specimen: but he really had no choice . . . or did he?

Chance a clue? 7 24

Choose your suspect:
Phoebus, p. 58
Peter Talgarth, p. 59

THE COVENT GARDEN MOB

There's no love lost among thieves, and finding a murderer proved tricky business.

1 Charlie "The Rat" Rainbird had terrorized the East End for 20 years without the police being able to do much about it.

2 The mere mention of his name was enough to strike fear in the hearts of his intended victims.

5 But somewhat strange was the lack of regret shown by Charlie's associates. Inspector Black was convinced that Charlie had been done in by one of his mob, and he set out to investigate. He soon learned the following:

#8074 BEAZLEY, TOM

#3740 MITCHELL, FRED

#7601 DEUTSCH, DUTCH

6 Tom Beazley, Fred Mitchell and the murderer had a special grudge against Charlie;

#2732 WEIDENFELD, MANNY

#4337 COLLINS, HARRY

#6532 FABER, DICK

7 "Dutch" Deutsch and Manny Weidenfeld knew that Charlie had had a secret "minder," and who he was;

8 On the night before the killing, Harry Collins, Dick Faber, Beazley, and the "minder" had lost heavily in a poker game at a Soho joint;

3 Even his cohorts treated him with the same respect one would show a snake – with which "The Rat" had much in common.

4 It was, therefore, with not much regret that the police greeted the news that Charlie's machine-gunned body had been found dumped in front of Stevens' Garage.

#1742 MACMILLAN, LUCKY

#6327 GOLLANCZ, CHICO

9 That "Lucky" MacMillan, Deutsch and the murderer had, the previous week, been refused a larger share of the profits by Charlie, and that "Lucky," Chico Gollancz and the murderer had failed to get the "minder" to kill Charlie;

10 Lastly, Inspector Black deduced that Collins, Faber and the killer were the ones who had it in most for Charlie.

11 Even when he got them all together, they refused to talk. But Inspector Black knew enough from his investigations to pinpoint the culprits.

???

Who was the minder, and who was the murderer?

Choose your suspect:

Tom Beazley, p. 55
Harry Collins, p. 55
"Dutch" Deutsch, p. 56
Dick Faber, p. 56

Chico Gollancz, p. 56
"Lucky" MacMillan, p. 57
Fred Mitchell, p. 58
Manny Weidenfeld, p. 59

INSIDE JOB

1 Inspector Black had been called in by the management of the Earthly Delights Transport Shipping Company over complaints about some missing goods.

In this case I took to heart the words of Inspector MacDonald – "You can take the boy out of the country, but you can't take the country out of the boy."

2 Guy Fakenham, the firm's chief executive, was able to give Black some information.

3 "It seems as though the missing items have turned up in America and every indication is that the guilty party has connections there. Moreover, since these losses have occurred only within the present year, after the company had expanded to meet demand, I believe the culprit is one of the newer employees."

4 "Well, there's a good place to start," said Black, "I'll interview the ones concerned."

5 Black kept the employment applications in front of him as he questioned the firm's three newest members.

6 Jonathan Mackie, a junior in the Accounting Department, seemed ill-at-ease at his interview. No, he hadn't noticed any irregularities in the accounts. What was Black suggesting–he only followed the orders of the head clerk.

EARTHLY DELIGHTS TRANSPORT SHIPPING CO
9 Upper Street,
Hendon-on-the-Hill

APPLICATION FOR EMPLOYMENT

Date of application 14/3/35

Name Jonathan Mackie

Address 2 Methley Street
Kennington, SE5

Age 23

Previously Employed by (Names and address of last two employers)
Mitchell Trading Company
35 Boulderstone Close
Seven Oaks, Kent

Beazley and Son
27 Trinity Court
London, SW3

Position desired Accounts Clerk

7 Had he ever been to the States? Yes, he'd been taken by his parents as a young child.

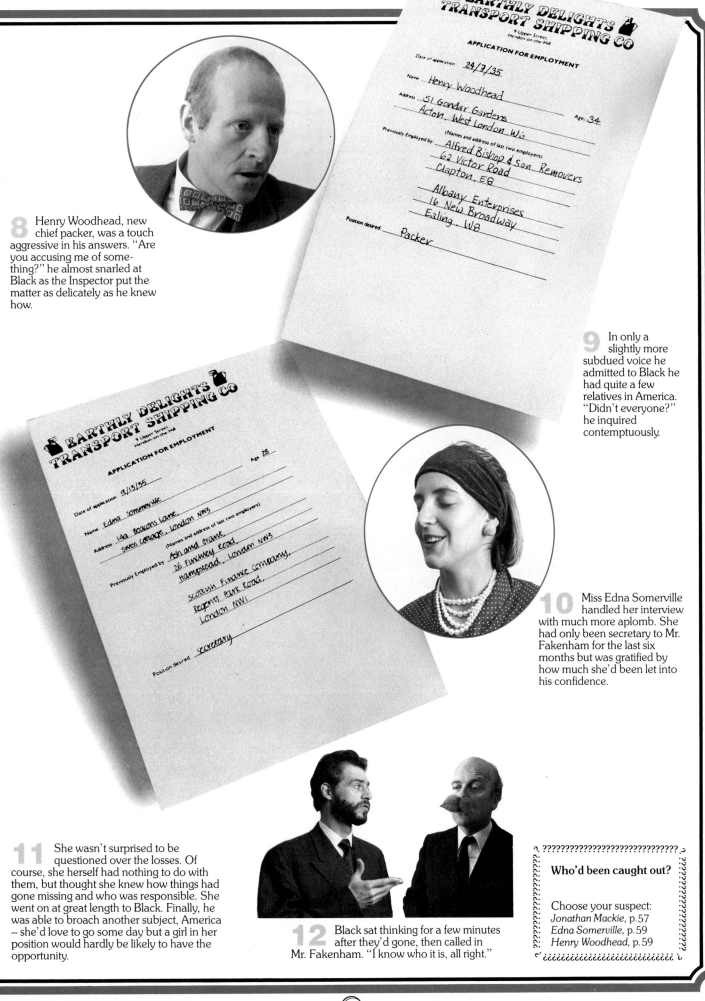

EARTHLY DELIGHTS TRANSPORT SHIPPING CO
9 Upper Street,
Hendon-on-the-Hill

APPLICATION FOR EMPLOYMENT

Date of application 24/7/35

Name Henry Woodhead

Address 51 Gondar Gardens   Age 34
Acton, West London W6

Previously Employed by
(Names and address of last two employers)
Alfred Bishop & Son Removers
62 Victor Road
Clapton, E8

Albany Enterprises
16 New Broadway
Ealing, W8

Position desired: Packer

8 Henry Woodhead, new chief packer, was a touch aggressive in his answers. "Are you accusing me of something?" he almost snarled at Black as the Inspector put the matter as delicately as he knew how.

9 In only a slightly more subdued voice he admitted to Black he had quite a few relatives in America. "Didn't everyone?" he inquired contemptuously.

EARTHLY DELIGHTS TRANSPORT SHIPPING CO
9 Upper Street,
Hendon-on-the-Hill

APPLICATION FOR EMPLOYMENT

Date of application 9/13/35   Age 28

Name Edna Somerville

Address 14a Beacons Lane,
Swiss Cottage, London NW3

(Names and address of last two employers)
Previously Employed by Ash and Frank,
26 Finchley Road,
Hampstead, London NW3

Scottish Finance Company,
Regents Park Road,
London NW1

Position desired: secretary

10 Miss Edna Somerville handled her interview with much more aplomb. She had only been secretary to Mr. Fakenham for the last six months but was gratified by how much she'd been let into his confidence.

11 She wasn't surprised to be questioned over the losses. Of course, she herself had nothing to do with them, but thought she knew how things had gone missing and who was responsible. She went on at great length to Black. Finally, he was able to broach another subject, America — she'd love to go some day but a girl in her position would hardly be likely to have the opportunity.

12 Black sat thinking for a few minutes after they'd gone, then called in Mr. Fakenham. "I know who it is, all right."

?????????????????????????????
Who'd been caught out?

Choose your suspect:
Jonathan Mackie, p.57
Edna Somerville, p.59
Henry Woodhead, p.59

HIGH STREET MURDER

A good officer must rely on evidence to prove guilt, an unsavoury background can only be a reference point.

1 Constable Nugent was known as much for his great height, as for his success in combatting street crime.

2 One day, while out patrolling in Paddington, he was killed by a bullet which entered his neck and lodged in his heart.

3 The nearby news vendor reported seeing an Austin sedan, registration WVP 47 near the scene of the crime.

4 Shortly after Nugent fell, a well-dressed young man had gotten out of the car, and had lost himself in the quickly gathering crowd.

5 Black traced the ownership of the car to "Lefty" Miller, a petty gangster well known to the police at Paddington Green.

6 He had a reluctant Lefty brought in for questioning. Lefty refused to identify the other fellow in his car and, in general, made few replies to Black's questions.

7 He did, however, volunteer a great deal of information on how he felt about the police, and those in Paddington, in particular.

8 Black was not amused. But in response to Lefty's request, handed him a cigarette...

10 Black turned to his constable and told him he'd have to do some more investigating before they could charge anyone.

9 ...and watched while the crook took a folder of matches from his pocket and lit it.

???

Who was the most likely culprit?

"Lefty" Miller, p. 57
His well-dressed friend, p. 59 or
Mr. X?, p. 57

Chance a clue? 14

¿¿¿

MARITAL MISHAP

A young wife's suicide is always distressing, but especially if there are suspicious circumstances.

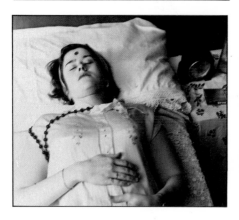

2 She was unconscious, but still alive when Inspector Black arrived with the ambulance. He watched as Mrs. Hutchinson was removed to hospital.

1 Hilda Ackroyd, maid to the Hutchinsons, was horrified to find her young mistress stretched out on her bed, a bullet in her head.

3 He asked the maid about the movements of the occupants of the flat. "There's just the two of them – Mr. and Mrs. Hutchinson." I come in and 'do' for them. I usually arrive before breakfast and leave after dinner.

4 "Yesterday, just before Mr. Hutchinson left to go out of town on business I heard them having a terrible row.

5 "I couldn't say for certain what it was about," she added virtuously, "but I think it was about him seeing another woman.

6 "At dinner Mrs. Hutchinson seemed pretty thoughtful, but didn't strike me as being about to kill herself."

7 Just then the 'phone rang. The maid answered. "Oh, Mr. Hutchinson, something terrible has happened. They just took poor mistress to Guy's Hospital, she's badly wounded. You'd better hurry to her . . ."

8 By the time Inspector Black took the 'phone Hutchinson had rung off.

9 Inspector Black made it to the hospital 5 minutes after Mrs. Hutchinson died, and only a minute or so before Mr. Hutchinson burst in.

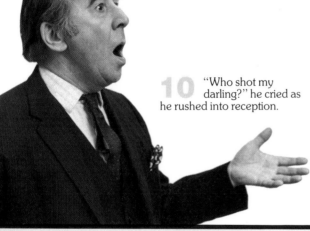

10 "Who shot my darling?" he cried as he rushed into reception.

11 "Just a minute there, Mr. Hutchinson," Black said, "I'd like to ask you some questions. Had your wife ever tried to commit suicide before? Had you quarrelled recently?"

12 "Well, once before I had to hide her sleeping draught after she threatened to drink all of it at once. And yesterday we did have a bit of an altercation over a trifle, but she seemed all right when I left."

???

Black had Hutchinson's movements confirmed. He'd been out of town all night. But Black still had to decide – did Mrs. Hutchinson do herself in, or had her husband helped her?

Chance a clue? 4 28

Choose your suspect:
Denise Hutchinson, p. 57
Theodore Hutchinson, p. 57

¿¿

TORCH SONG TRAGEDY

This was one of those cases I could tell at first glance didn't take all that much looking into.

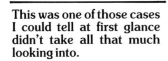

1 Thelma Porter, chanteuse at Jimmy's, the Soho nightclub, maintained her innocence over the death of her long-time admirer, Tony Morani. He'd been found shot dead at close range in his "office."

2 Thelma had been spotted leaving the building where Morani had his "office" early on the morning he turned up dead. But she was able to explain her presence there to Inspector Black as follows:

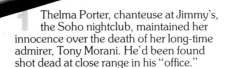

3 Morani had thrown her over for another woman – some dumb blonde in a chorus line – and had stopped the payments on her flat.

4 Thelma felt Morani owed her something and she was going to make sure she got it. She knew he normally had a big poker game once a month, and rarely came away a loser.

5 Rather than ask for the money since she knew he'd turn her down – she decided to discover where he'd stashed it, then "borrow" it at a later time.

7 He turned on the light, but just as she got to the door, he shut and locked it. "I looked through the keyhole but couldn't see anything."

6 Therefore, she waited for him late that Friday until he appeared about 3.30 the next morning. She followed him noiselessly down the dark hall before he entered his room.

9 Thelma looked at Black from under her eyelashes – "of course I am, I saw a light under the door." She continued to tell him how she waited in the hall for another 15-20 minutes hoping he'd come out when she heard a shot from inside.

8 Black fingered the blood-stained key found in Morani's room and asked his only question: "Are you certain he turned on the light?"

11 "As far as the money goes, I can only say I have no idea where it is, and as for poor Tony – he either shot himself in remorse for what he'd done to me, or maybe that dumb blonde wasn't so dumb after all!"

10 "I decided not to hang around to see who came out and was finding my way home when your constable insisted I come with him to the Station.

12 Black checked up on Morani's new friend, Stella Asky, who although she hadn't a verifiable alibi for the time in question, fervently denied she had anything to do with his death.

?????????????????????????????
Black had a lot to think about – two beautiful murder suspects, or a suicide . . .

Chance a clue? 1 35

Choose your suspect:
Stella Asky, p. 55
Tony Morani, p. 58
Thelma Porter, p. 58

A WINTER'S TALE

Jealousy has often proved a man's, and a woman's, undoing . . .

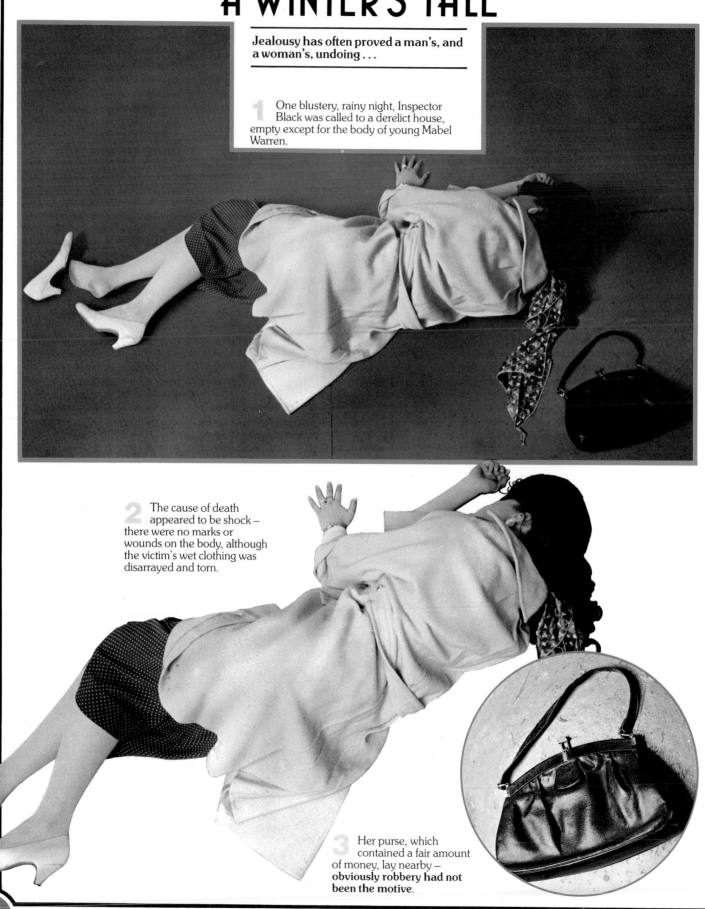

1 One blustery, rainy night, Inspector Black was called to a derelict house, empty except for the body of young Mabel Warren.

2 The cause of death appeared to be shock – there were no marks or wounds on the body, although the victim's wet clothing was disarrayed and torn.

3 Her purse, which contained a fair amount of money, lay nearby – **obviously robbery had not been the motive.**

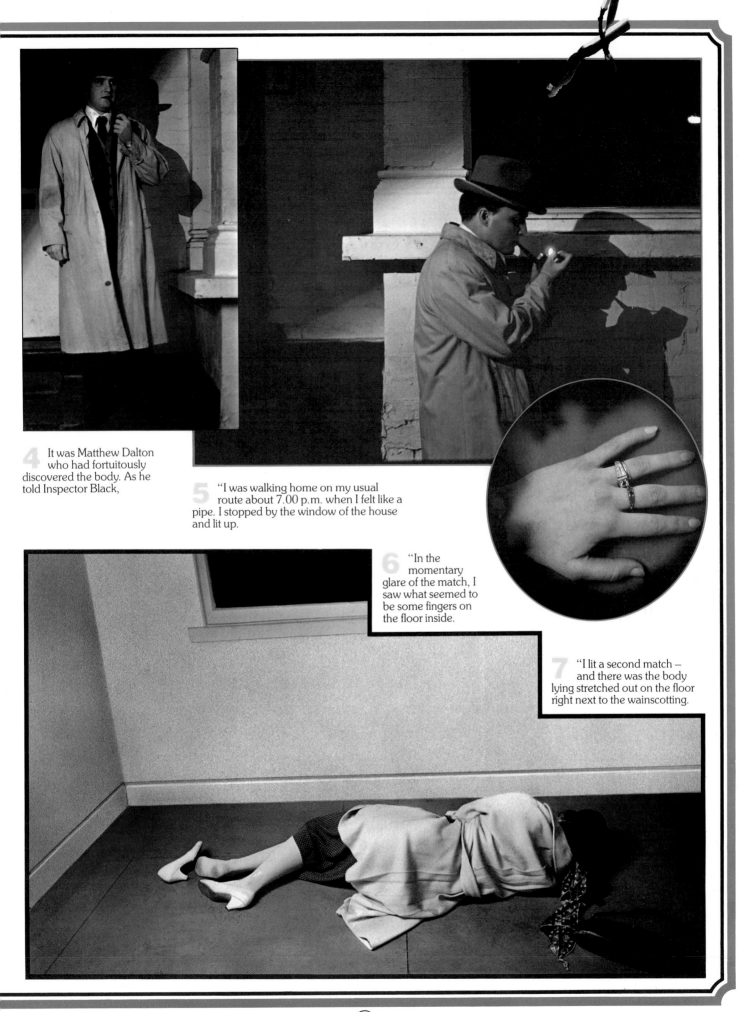

4 It was Matthew Dalton who had fortuitously discovered the body. As he told Inspector Black,

5 "I was walking home on my usual route about 7.00 p.m. when I felt like a pipe. I stopped by the window of the house and lit up.

6 "In the momentary glare of the match, I saw what seemed to be some fingers on the floor inside.

7 "I lit a second match — and there was the body lying stretched out on the floor right next to the wainscotting.

8 "It's a good thing I didn't stop to light my pipe in the doorway or I never would have seen the body.

9 "I saw some other people hurrying home in the storm and I called to them to help me. Then I turned to go inside. The door had been forced already and was banging with the wind.

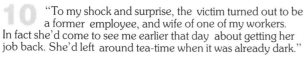

10 "To my shock and surprise, the victim turned out to be a former employee, and wife of one of my workers. In fact she'd come to see me earlier that day about getting her job back. She'd left around tea-time when it was already dark."

11 Adela Mason, Mr. Dalton's secretary, was rung up at home and confirmed Mabel Warren's presence in the office that day. She claimed to have heard her say that Mr. Warren had been against her asking for her old job back. That didn't surprise Miss Mason as Mabel had once been Mr. Dalton's secretary, and some said she'd been more than that. Everyone had thought she married Warren on the rebound, and it was common knowledge he was jealous of Mr. Dalton.

12 Mr. Warren was not at home when Inspector Black arrived to tell him of his wife's death.

13 On a subsequent call he could not give a satisfactory explanation of his movements that day. He said he and his wife had quarrelled at breakfast over her wanting to get her old job back. He felt he earned sufficient for the two. He'd left the house shortly after she stormed out.

14 He'd been very upset about the situation and had thought about having it out with Mr. Dalton. However, he'd decided to cool down a bit before attempting an interview, and had spent the day doing that.

15 Inspector Black had a lot to think about. Mr. Warren's story was far from satisfactory, but Mr. Dalton had also said some curious things.

??

Had an unknown party been the perpetrator or had he already the culprit to hand?

Chance a clue? 9

Choose your suspect:
Mr. Dalton, p. 56
Mr. Warren, p. 59
Mr. X, p. 56

¿¿

SECRETS OF THE DEEP

Forensic science is of great use in detecting, but often it just confirms what one's instincts have seized upon.

1 Inspector Black was summoned one day to Rotherhithe to investigate a rather gruesome ocurrence.

2 Tom Bell, a neighbourhood character, who often slept rough, had pulled from the Thames a chest containing the decomposed remains of a young woman.

REPORT OF MISSING PERSON

Name: Vanessa Tarlton
Address: 47 Cholmley Gardens, West Hampstead

Appearance:
Height: 5'4"
Weight: 8 st.
Hair colour: Brown
Eye colour: Blue
Distinguishing characteristics: Mole on left shoulder
Clothes when last seen: Grey dress, black shoes, blue coat and blue hat

Date: 25/2/36
Time: 9:25 a.m.

Last sighting: 23/2/36
Reported by: Peter Tarlton
Address: as above

Relationship to missing person: Husband

3 The condition of the woman was so bad all Black had to go on was the victim's clothes. Luckily these seemed to match those of Vanessa Tarlton, reported missing several months earlier.

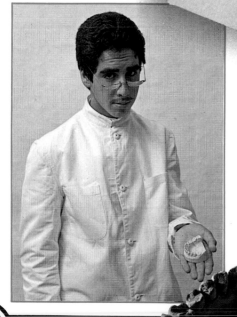

4 Vanessa's dentist identified her remains through dental records . . .

5 . . . and the coroner identified the means of her death – a stab wound in the heart.

6 It was with some interest, therefore, that Black interviewed the far from grieving husband. Peter Tarlton claimed that his wife had often spoken to him about a divorce, and although he had reported her missing, he hadn't been unduly alarmed when she had disappeared.

7 In fact, he'd met another woman some time ago whom he wanted to marry, and if Vanessa hadn't turned up soon, he would have filed for divorce.

9 Black learned that Bell was well-known around the neighbourhood for scavenging from the river and that people thought him a bit "queer".

8 Black returned to have a few further words with Bell. He repeated his story of spying the floating chest from the shoreline, and having dragged it ashore.

Black wasn't convinced of his guilt, but he was certain that one of the two men knew more than he was telling. Which of the two did he suspect?

Chance a clue? 15 38

Choose your suspect:
Tom Bell, p. 57
Peter Tarlton, p. 59

QUARREL AT THE QUARRY

Love seemed to be at the centre of this situation, but death put an end to that.

1 Inspector Black had been called out to Ryan's Quarry to investigate the death of Joseph May.

2 The body was not a pretty sight. It lay as it had fallen, a gash in the head. The knife that caused it lay open near the feet.

3 The collar of May's jacket and his tightly-fitting cap were smeared with blood from a bullet hole at the base of the skull.

4 Black turned to Jack Cutler, the man who claimed to have killed May in self-defence, "Let's hear your story . . ."

5 "Joe and I had been mates for a long time, since we met at the Quarry."

To Joe
Love Lilly xo

To Jack
Love Lilly xo

6 "However, we both fell for the same woman, Lily Davies, who was Joe's girl for a while, then mine."

8 "I thought I'd better carry a gun, just in case. Today, the other fellows had gone off to the pub but I wanted to earn some extra.

9 "Joe came back and got fairly nasty over Lily. Insisted I stop seeing her. I refused. All of a sudden he sprang at me with his knife.

7 "Joe became rather jealous. He kept making threatening remarks, I didn't feel safe about him.

10 "There was nothing I could do. I reached for my gun and shot him. You don't think I would have killed him if it wasn't in self-defence, do you?"

11 Black accompanied the body to the morgue. The pathologist set about examining the body, and started by removing a piece of May's cap from the wound at the nape of the neck.

12 Black knew that May's prints were on the knife, but did that necessarily confirm Cutler's story?

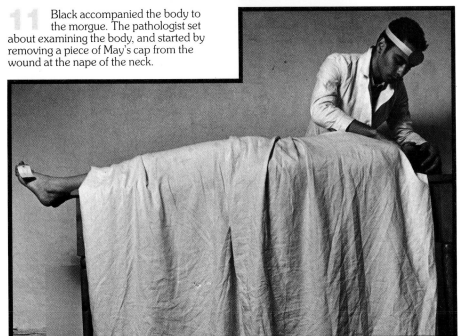

??

Self-defence or cold-blooded murder?

Chance a clue? 11 32

Choose your suspect:
May, p. 57
Cutler, p. 55

DRESSED TO KILL

A confusing case, this, but thanks to the constable's keen eye, one which proved eminently solvable.

1 J. Hartley Plummer, owner of two of Saville Row's better suitors establish-ments, was found dead in his car in a little mews a couple of streets from his shop.

2 He was well known as a hard taskmaster to his staff, and lived over one of his premises so as to keep well in touch.

3 Plummer had had more dignity in life than in death. It was the car's open door with its unrestricted view of the driver's socks and shoes which had first caught the eye of a passing bobby.

4 He'd then taken a closer look – and saw the blood which had seeped from the victim's mouth onto the collar of his striped shirt and light coloured suit.

5 The dead man's watch was smashed – its hands had stopped at 7.45.

6 It was now 1.15 but it looked as though the driver had been dead for more than 5 hours.

7 It also looked as if the person had been a victim of a hit and run driver. Blood on the road next to the car and up along the seat seemed to indicate he'd been hit and had then attempted to get into the car – perhaps to drive for help?

8 The constable rang through his unpleasant findings to Black, who ascertained it was Plummer, who had been reported missing earlier that morning by his long-time girlfriend, Désirée MacIntyre.

9 The well-known model had told Black she'd expected Plummer at around 8 the previous evening. They'd had a dinner date at Cafe des Artistes.

10 When he didn't show by 9 she became quite annoyed, and thinking she'd been stood up, arranged for another of her male friends to take her out.

11 At the restaurant she was introduced to Todd Burgess, Plummer's new shop manager, who said he'd been with his employer up until 6.30 when Plummer had left to get ready for his date with Miss MacIntyre. Burgess made everyone laugh with his stories of how Plummer despaired over Burgess' lack of taste and only kept him on because he was good with customers.

13 Black, therefore, knew something about the case when the constable rang. He asked him a few questions about the driver's appearance and listened gravely to the constable's theory of a hit-and-run.

12 Miss MacIntyre's new companions proved so engaging she soon forgot about Plummer, until she was rung by Burgess the next morning to be told that Plummer had not come into work – an *extremely* unusual occurrence. She, then, had rung Inspector Black.

??

"It's going to be simpler than that," said Black. And then he told him how to go about finding the guilty party.

Chance a clue? 16 20

Choose your suspect:
Hit and run driver, p.56
Désirée MacIntyre, p.57
Todd Burgess, p.55

¿¿

DARING DEATH

I've never been one for the supernatural — most of the "strange" occurrences I've come across have been rooted in reality.

1 Inspector Black was summoned to Wintlesham Hall to investigate the tragic death of Christopher Morham.

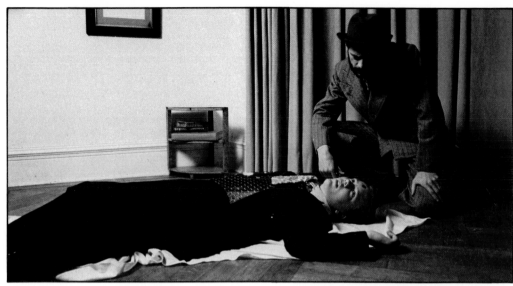

2 The body lay in the hall beneath one of the family portraits. The face bore a peculiar expression.

3 Inspector Black pulled the bed sheet from beneath the body and noted the single bullet hole, quite close to the bottom of the sheet. There were no powder burns.

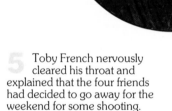

4 He turned and looked searchingly at the three men crowded around.

5 Toby French nervously cleared his throat and explained that the four friends had decided to go away for the weekend for some shooting.

6 "I knew about this place," interrupted Ben Bennet. "It has quite a history. Last night at dinner I mentioned that there was a resident ghost."

7 French gave a slight shudder and continued. "When I heard that, I told the others that the mere thought of a ghost was enough to unnerve me, and that I'd shoot if I saw one. They all laughed saying no real ghost would be frightened by bullets. Anyhow, they all knew my hand gun only held blanks!

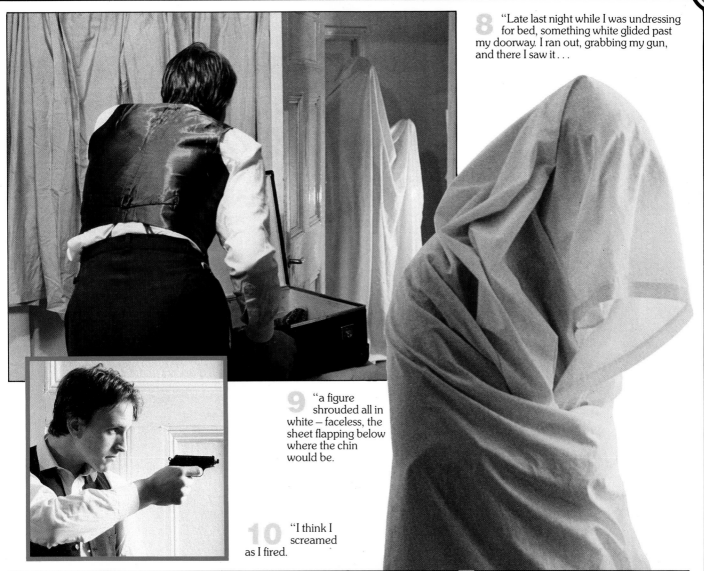

8 "Late last night while I was undressing for bed, something white glided past my doorway. I ran out, grabbing my gun, and there I saw it . . .

9 "a figure shrouded all in white – faceless, the sheet flapping below where the chin would be.

10 "I think I screamed as I fired.

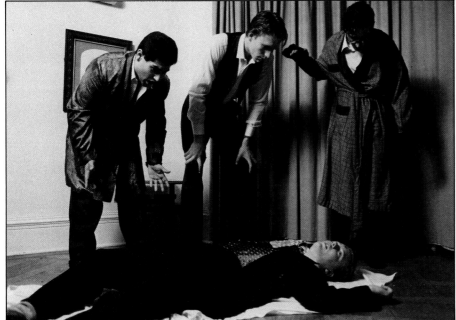

11 "The others ran out of their rooms. John, here, turned back the sheet, under it was Chris – he was dead – a bullet through his forehead. Someone must have replaced my blanks with live cartridges!"

12 Black looked around. "Was that window open at the time?" he asked. Upon getting an affirmative answer he then added, "This was no accident, this was murder!"

What made Black so certain of his claim?

Chance a clue? 18

Choose your suspect:
Mr. X, p.58
Toby French, p. 56
One of the other 2, p.59

REPAIRING FENCES

1 Inspector Black had had little success in recovering the Carroll pearls. The magnificent strand, conservatively worth £5,000, had been missing at least four months.

2 Suspicion centred on Billy Bond, a well-known fence, specialising in the jewellery trade.

3 The police had kept Billy's house under surveillance since the robbery but had not been able to gather enough evidence to allow them to seek a search warrant.

4 "If we're going to search that house, Coombes," Black told his young constable, "we shall have to don some disguise."

5 A short while later two inspectors from the Water Board turned up at Bond's claiming a serious leakage had been traced to the premises.

6 Not surprisingly, Mr. Bond didn't seem all that glad to see them. "There's no leakage here," he claimed. "We'll be the judge of that," said the older of the two inspectors.

7 The men from the Water Board were very diligent in their search – looking in even the least likely spot for water pipes.

8 But although Mr. Bond seemed anxious for their exit, especially when nothing untoward turned up, the inspectors were eager to have one last go, and set off for the old outside water closet.

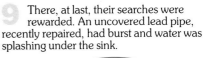

9 There, at last, their searches were rewarded. An uncovered lead pipe, recently repaired, had burst and water was splashing under the sink.

10 "Well I guess that's it," Bond said with a sickly grin as he stared at the pipe. You'd better turn it off at the main while we call the plumber," said the inspector.

11 "We'd better hurry," said Black to Coombes as they made their escape. "I imagine we've only got about 10 minutes to change out of these clothes into our uniforms and be back to nab both Bond and the pearls."

12 In fact, it was more like fifteen minutes later that Bond was caught red-handed trying to hide the pearls in the back garden.

???

How did Black know he was going to make the attempt?

Chance a clue? 12 34
1 Where had Bond hidden the pearls?
2 How did Black know?
Answer see truth " J",
¿¿

TOO CLOSE A SHAVE

I was a whisker away from nabbing the wrong subject, but then I remembered that primary police dictum – motive and opportunity!

1 Evelyn Hardcastle, manicurist at Monsieur Gaston's Salon, arrived late to find her employer lying in a welter of blood.

CLOSED

2 Monsieur Gaston, a.k.a. Roger Promfret, had been murdered by a sharp instrument which had severed his jugular vein. Evelyn put a *closed* sign out and rang Inspector Black.

3 He sent his constable to make enquiries and then began his investigations. He glanced briefly at the appointments book – no one expected for another hour – then at the open manicure set near the body. Finally he stooped to pick something up – **a blood-stained safety razor blade.**

4 "This could have done it all right," he said, then turned to ask Miss Hardcastle about her employer. "He was a bit of a phoney – though there was no harm in him. While he bragged a lot about his conquests, the only women who took to him were mainly inexperienced shop girls impressed by his accent."

5 The constable returned – nobody had been seen entering or leaving the shop before Miss Hardcastle – and there were several witnesses to the fact. "Looks like it's an inside job, Sir."

6 Gaston's Salon was one of two shops in the converted house. In addition to the salon there was a barber's and several flats. Black tried the barber's first.

7 The barber was Sicilian and obviously no friend of Gaston's. "Monsieur Gaston, pah!" Gaston had never set foot in his shop, had snubbed him. "Il diavolo, he deserved to die!"

8 Upstairs were three flats. In the first were two clerks. Bert Green, the first to appear, told Black Gaston was a great one for the ladies and a bit of a snob. He'd taken Bob's girl to dinner then dropped her. She hadn't been grand enough for him, nor was Emma, the seamstress next door. The roommate had been upset ever since his girl had turned him down.

9 "Either one of you chaps use a safety razor?" asked Black.

10 Neither did, and neither had gone out last night. They had heard one other person in the bathroom – could have been Miss Dean or the "upstairs". Both had slept late.

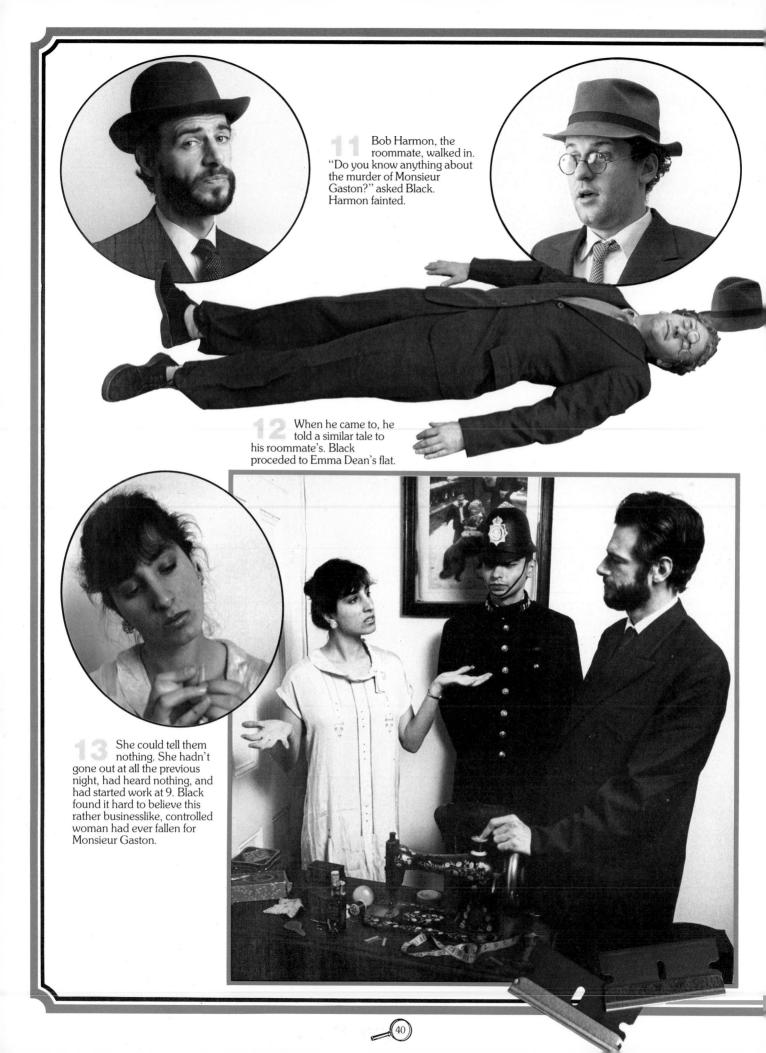

11 Bob Harmon, the roommate, walked in. "Do you know anything about the murder of Monsieur Gaston?" asked Black. Harmon fainted.

12 When he came to, he told a similar tale to his roommate's. Black proceded to Emma Dean's flat.

13 She could tell them nothing. She hadn't gone out at all the previous night, had heard nothing, and had started work at 9. Black found it hard to believe this rather businesslike, controlled woman had ever fallen for Monsieur Gaston.

14 The illustrator was still asleep when they got to his flat. Ted Wilson had been to a late-night party and hadn't heard a thing till Black banged at the door. He didn't look surprised when Black told him why he was there.

15 Black walked over to the table covered with his drawing equipment. "Use these a lot in your work?" Black inquired casually.

16 "As a matter of fact I do. I use them to cut out drawings. Don't tell me Gaston was done in with one of those!" he said mockingly.

17 But that's just what Black did tell him. Then he stepped outside and conferred with his constable.

???

Five suspects, each of whom might have killed Gaston, but which one did?

Chance a clue? 17 22 31

Choose your suspect:
Emma Dean, p. 56   *Enrico Rampardi*, p. 58
Bert Green, p. 56   *Ted Wilson*, p. 59
Bob Harmon, p. 56

THE TAKING OF LITTLE ZOË

Tug-of-love situations require the utmost delicacy in their handling. Careful study of the evidence pointed me in the right direction.

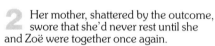

2 Her mother, shattered by the outcome, swore that she'd never rest until she and Zoë were together once again.

1 The Pettit divorce case had occupied the front pages of the papers for several weeks. Finally, the case was decided in favour of the plaintiff. He was also allowed custody of the only child of the union – little Zoë.

3 In the meantime, the child lived at her father's estate, Hilltop Lodge, and was cared for by her devoted nanny, Eloise.

4 One afternoon Randolph Pettit received a devastating telephone call . . . little Zoë had disappeared.

5 He rushed home to find a considerably shaken Eloise being comforted by Inspector Black. She relayed the following.

6 "I took little Zoë into the back garden where we played hide 'n' seek. I stood near the shed to cover my eyes while she found a hiding place. Most often she hid in the shed itself.

7 "The last time it was her turn I waited a few minutes and then went to look for her. As I got to the door of the shed, someone pushed me inside and locked it.

9 Carter had a little more to add – he'd heard what sounded like a large motor car going down the back road not far from the shed, but had been too slow to see the car, or even the direction it travelled.

8 "I screamed and pounded on the door for several minutes and at last, Carter, the gardener, heard me and set me free. But little Zoë was gone."

10 Pettit turned to Black. "It must be Amelia," he said, "She swore she'd have little Zoë. I want you to find them, but I want you to be discreet. If you call in your men, it'll be all over the front pages again."

11 "Then, there's no time to lose," shouted Black. He knew the back road lead south to the airfield and north to the steamship port. "We've got to see which way the kidnappers went."

12 While Pettit brought his car round, Black rushed out to the back road. He kneeled and stared at the fresh tracks made by the studded tyres in the soft road.

13 "Let's go," he yelled as he saw Pettit's car. "We'll probably just have enough time to stop them if I'm right about the direction."

???

But which way did they go? North towards the port or south towards the airfield?

Chance a clue? 6 25

Answer see "K"

DEADLY HOBBY

Visits to exotic locales are not part of an ordinary copper's life, but solving this crime was a matter of home-grown common sense!

1 Roger Devereaux of the Bombay Boutique Company had been born and raised in India where he had first experienced his fondness for snakes.

2 He'd returned to England to help manage the trading company. Accompanying him on his journey to his new quarters was a large poisonous snake.

3 "Tillie," as he called the snake, lived in a long box with a glass top which was normally fitted with a strong lock; Mr. Devereaux kept the key in his pocket.

4 But on the morning that Isobel Hutton, Mr. Devereaux's maid, discovered his dead body, the box was wide open and Tillie was loose in the room.

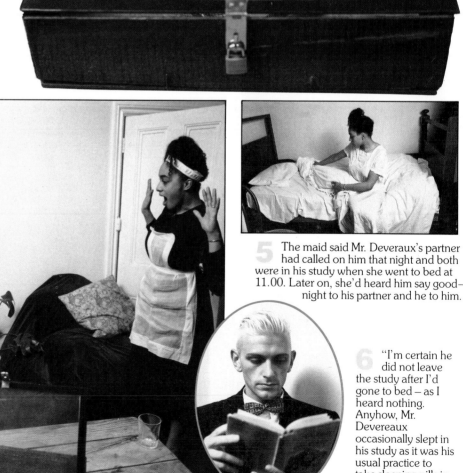

5 The maid said Mr. Deveraux's partner had called on him that night and both were in his study when she went to bed at 11.00. Later on, she'd heard him say good-night to his partner and he to him.

6 "I'm certain he did not leave the study after I'd gone to bed – as I heard nothing. Anyhow, Mr. Devereaux occasionally slept in his study as it was his usual practice to take sleeping pills in his milk."

7 The maid went on to say the snake box had been locked when she brought in Devereaux's milk at half past 10 the night before. "I hated that thing and wouldn't come into the room if she wasn't locked in."

8 Mr. Stanley Trilby, Devereaux's childhood friend and current business partner, had been contacted to deal with the snake.

9 He was very upset about his partner's death but agreed to attempt to put the snake back in her box while the police watched from outside.

10 Without hesitating he grabbed Tillie by the neck, carried her over to her box and shut her up inside. Then he piled a number of books on the top.

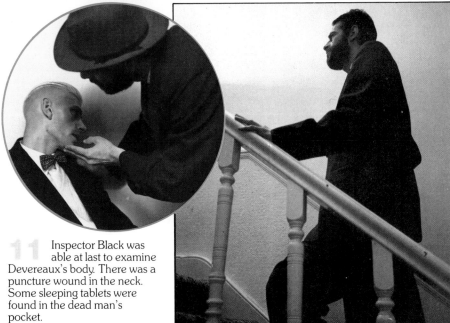

11 Inspector Black was able at last to examine Devereaux's body. There was a puncture wound in the neck. Some sleeping tablets were found in the dead man's pocket.

12 "Devereaux must have let Tillie out of her box after his guest had gone with disastrous consequences," thought Black. "But I'm not satisfied. I'd better have a look upstairs."

13 Black stood by Devereaux's night table and searched the drawers. At last he gave a satisfied grunt. He'd found what he was looking for.

???

"Now to deal with the responsible party," thought Black. Who was that?

Chance a clue? 3 29 36

Choose your suspect:
Isobel Hutton, p. 57
Tillie, p. 59
Stanley Trilby, p. 59

PEMBROKE'S POSER

The circumstances here certainly seemed desperate, but were they enough to lead to suicide?

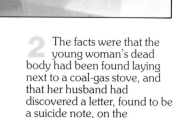

1 The police, investigating the death of Agatha Pembroke, were not satisfied with the evidence that had been uncovered so far.

2 The facts were that the young woman's dead body had been found laying next to a coal-gas stove, and that her husband had discovered a letter, found to be a suicide note, on the mantlepiece in their bedroom.

The husband's story

5 The front door had been locked and she was not in the sitting room or dining room.

4 He'd been alarmed at her absence and had gone downstairs to find her. She had not answered when he called her name.

3 Mr. Pembroke claimed to have woken up to find his wife missing from their bed. Due to his blindness, he couldn't say at what time exactly.

6 It was only on opening the kitchen door that he smelt gas, and subsequently stumbled on her body.

7 He believed her suicide was the result of the strain of having to care for him. Though he still went to his office for part of the day, he had lost his sight six months previously.

8 Since that event they'd had frequent quarrels over small things. "Only the previous day, while attempting to open the kitchen door, I'd scattered all my loose change over the floor. After Agatha picked up the money and gave it to me, I told her that a shilling was missing. She furiously denied it and we had a real row. But later on, she did find it had rolled under the kitchen door."

9 Other witnesses mentioned that the couple's friend, Mr. Alan Holland, was a frequent visitor at the house. Mr. Holland claimed that the Pembrokes had not been on good terms even before he had lost his sight.

10 Mr. Pembroke denied any previous estrangement, and said his wife had complained of Holland's frequent attentions.

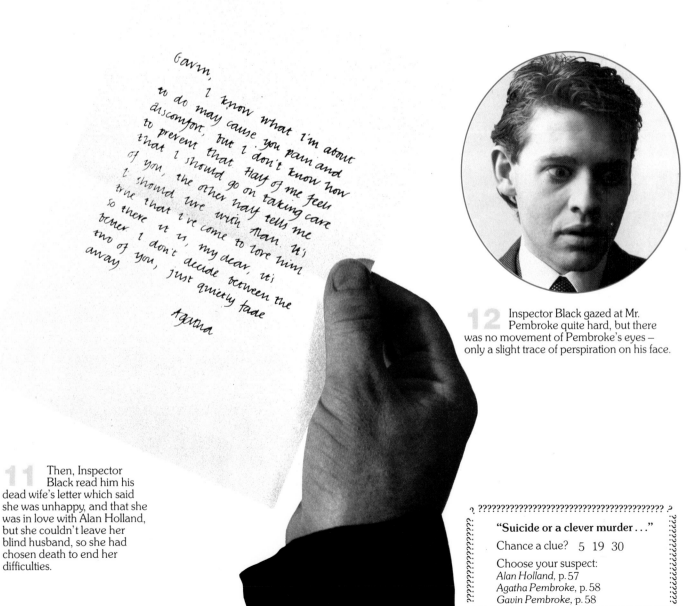

Gavin,

I know what I'm about to do may cause you pain and discomfort, but I don't know how to prevent that. Half of me feels that I should go on taking care of you, the other half tells me I should live with Alan. It's true that I've come to love him so there it is, my dear, it's better. I don't decide between the two of you, just quietly fade away.

Agatha

12 Inspector Black gazed at Mr. Pembroke quite hard, but there was no movement of Pembroke's eyes — only a slight trace of perspiration on his face.

11 Then, Inspector Black read him his dead wife's letter which said she was unhappy, and that she was in love with Alan Holland, but she couldn't leave her blind husband, so she had chosen death to end her difficulties.

???

"Suicide or a clever murder . . ."

Chance a clue?   5   19   30

Choose your suspect:
Alan Holland, p. 57
Agatha Pembroke, p. 58
Gavin Pembroke, p. 58

A PROBLEM OF SECURITY

Cases involving national security rarely come my way, but solving this one required no special skills.

1 Reports of Gregory Miller's new fuel had reached the ears of the defense ministry. Four men were sent out to evaluate and purchase the secret formula. Three travelled by train; one motored down to the country.

2 They were impressed by the security provisions of the scientist's laboratory and special sleeping quarters – there were bars on all the windows.

3 The five spent a pleasant evening before the fire in the main house while rain beat at the windows. At about 11.30, Dr. Miller retired to his sleeping quarters in the laboratory.

4 By the time John Parker arrived downstairs for breakfast the others, and two policemen were already there. Dr. Miller had been murdered, and his secret formula stolen.

5 Several unusual features about the case prompted the police to interview the men separately.

Each denied he had anything to do with the case, and all were asked to sign their names and empty their pockets. Steven Curtis proved to be left-handed.

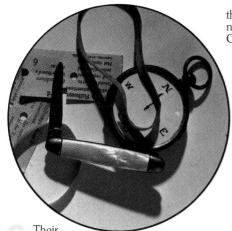

7 Curtis had two packets of matches, three of Dr. Miller's best cigars, a small camera and a betting slip.

6 Their belongings contained some curious items. Gordon Carroll's pockets had held a couple of elastic bands, two underground tickets, a compass and a small pocket knife.

8 From David Joiner's pocket issued a fountain pen, small account book, two white feathers and a pocket dictionary.

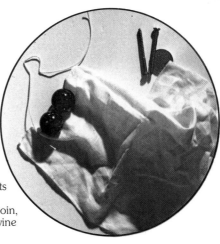

9 John Parker's pockets held a crumpled handkerchief, a Chinese coin, some screws, a piece of twine and two marbles.

10 None of their other belongings — pyjamas, clothes, wallets — contained the missing formula, which had run to a couple of pages.

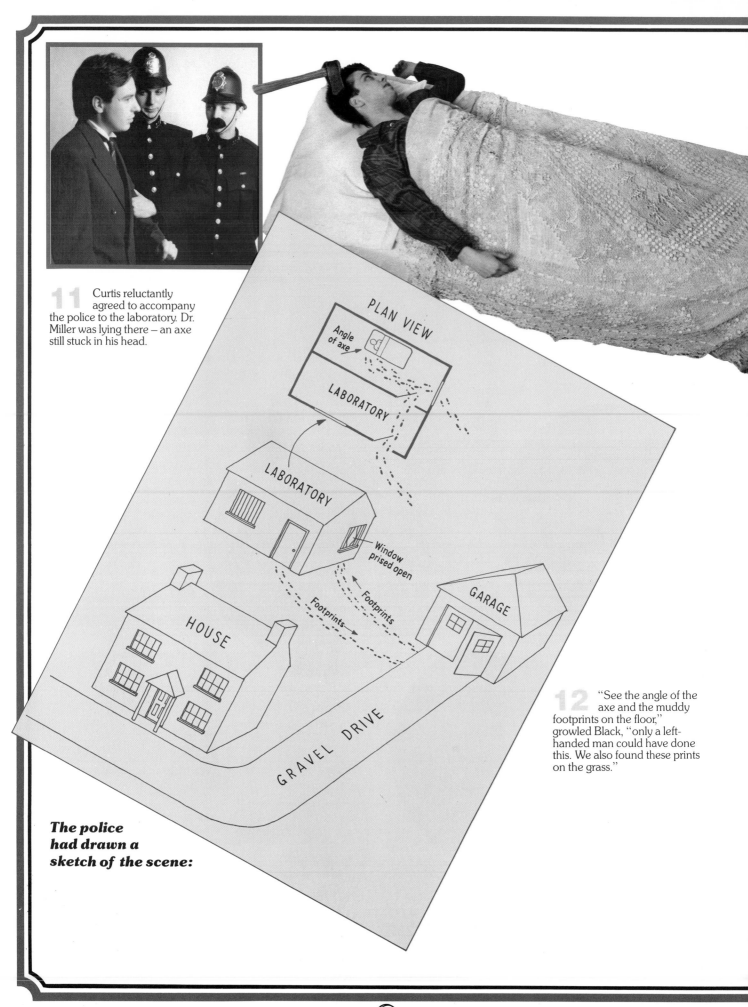

11 Curtis reluctantly agreed to accompany the police to the laboratory. Dr. Miller was lying there – an axe still stuck in his head.

PLAN VIEW

Angle of axe →

LABORATORY

LABORATORY

Window prised open

Footprints

Footprints

HOUSE

GARAGE

GRAVEL DRIVE

12 "See the angle of the axe and the muddy footprints on the floor," growled Black, "only a left-handed man could have done this. We also found these prints on the grass."

The police had drawn a sketch of the scene:

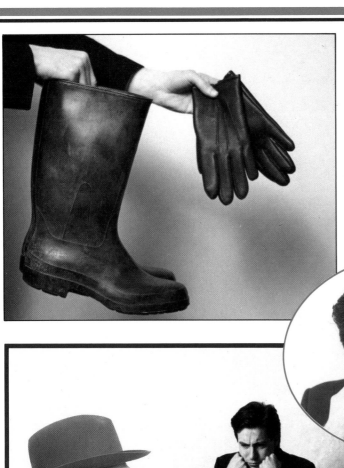

13 Curtis was shown also the pair of muddy wellingtons that had made the prints and a pair of wet gloves, known to be Carroll's. "But we don't suspect him. You didn't leave any fingerprints, but we have more than enough evidence to put you behind bars for life."

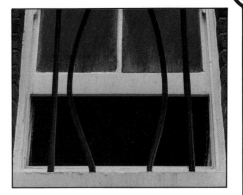

14 Curtis was showing signs of desperation. These increased as he was shown the prised-apart bars of the laboratory windows.

15 "I couldn't have done this," he stammered. "You can search me and my room but you won't find anything. I'm innocent I tell you."

16 Curtis was taken back to the house where he was questioned for a number of hours. His ordeal was interrupted by a phone call for Inspector Black.

17 A constable from a neighbouring town reported that a local farmer out hunting had discovered something curious which turned out to be the formula.

18 "Well, this puts a new light on things," said Black.

???

"I not only know who did it, but how it was done."

Chance a clue? 13   26   37

Choose your suspect:
Gordon Carroll, p. 55
Steven Curtis, p. 55
David Joiner, p. 57
John Parker, p. 58

ILL MET BY MOONLIGHT

I had an eye witness to this crime, but would the testimony of one so young pass muster in an adult world?

2 Sobbed Annabel, "See, the money is not where I left it, the piggy bank is empty."

1 Mrs. Postlewaite was disturbed early one morning by her little Annabel crying about how her carefully hoarded pound notes had gone missing.

3 Rupert, Annabel's older brother, not only denied taking the money, but said something which further disturbed Mrs. Postlewaite. He claimed one of the maids had taken it and that he'd **seen** her.

[Floor plan]

Sundrenched wall in garden

N
W · E
S

Window

Stairs

Door open

RUPERT'S ROOM

ANNABEL'S ROOM

Window

Window

4 "I was so hot last night, Mummy, that I kept my door open, so I'd feel the breeze from the hall window, though there was a lot of light from the moon.

Original drawing from the files of Inspector Black...

5 "It may have been that or something else that woke me. But as I lay awake for a few minutes a shadow appeared on the wall opposite. I turned over thinking it was only Rose or Emily, probably coming back from the toilet downstairs.

6 "I woke up though when I heard Annabel crying next door. She told me her money was gone. I remembered at once about seeing one of the maids."

7 The two girls summoned from their attic room wondered why they were being called downstairs. "Maybe Madam's upset over another of Rupert's pranks," suggested Emily. "Could be she wants to discuss plans for the children's summer holidays," said Rose.

8 The last thing they expected to hear, and which both vigorously denied, was having taken the money.

9 Nor would either girl admit she'd left their room. "We were together all night, Madam," they swore.

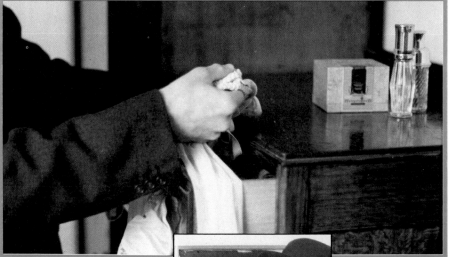

10 Mrs. Postlewaite was determined to get to the bottom of the problem and rang for Inspector Black. He listened to the maids' evidence, searched their attic room but found nothing;

12 then entered Rupert's room. He searched all the likely places but found no money.

11 glanced for a moment out of the hall window at the sun-drenched walled garden on his right,

13 But Black was not discouraged. "Have to get up pretty early in the morning to fool me," he muttered.

????????????????????????????????

Who was he referring to?

Chance a clue? 10 23

Choose your suspect:
Rose Barker, p.55
Emily Douglas, p.56
Rupert Postlewaite, p.58

THE CLUES

?1 Who locked the door?
Lose 15 points.

?2 Plenty more where that came from?
Lose 20 points.

?3 Locked-up case?
Lose 10 points.

?4 Eternal sleep? No, infernal red herring!
Lose 20 points.

?5 Loose change.
Lose 10 points.

?6 "Carter . . . heard what sounded like a large motor car . . ." Lose 10 points.

?7 Curses! Soiled again.
Lose 20 points.

?8 Buried treasure?
Lose 20 points.

?9 A light in the storm?
Lose 15 points.

?10 The shadow knows . . . or does it? Red herring.
Lose 10 points.

?11 Who's lying?
Lose 15 points.

?12 A revealing leak.
Lose 15 points.

?13 Not an easy job.
Lose 10 points.

?14 P.C. Nugent had been in good standing in the force.
Lose 20 points.

?15 A problem of decay?
Lose 15 points.

?16 Match for no man.
Lose 15 points.

?17 A sharp tongue, and a red herring. Lose 10 points.

?18 Holey shroud.
Lose 15 points.

?19 An open door?
Lose 10 points.

?20 Does she need to come clean? Lose 15 points.

?21 Sheds no light on the case.
Red herring.
Lose 20 points.

?22 A real cut-up?
No, a red herring.
Lose 10 points.

?23 Map mishap?
Lose 10 points.

?24 Was Barnabas bitten or smitten?
Lose 20 points.

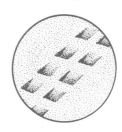

?25 Making tracks.
Lose 10 points.

?26 Perfect picture – of a red herring.
Lose 10 points.

?27 A matter of much gravity.
Lose 20 points.

?28 Was it something he said?
Lose 20 points.

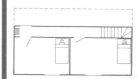

?29 Hard to handle?
Lose 10 points.

?30 What's cooking?
Lose 10 points.

?31 Tools of her trade.
Lose 10 points.

?32 Spring ahead, or fall back?
Lose 15 points.

THE SUSPECTS

?33

More gin than rummy?
No, a red herring.
Lose 20 points.

?34

Fancy dresser?
No, a red herring.
Lose 15 points.

?35

Left in the dark?
Lose 15 points.

?36

A sleep inducer?
Lose 10 points.

?37

Only a feather-weight
could have taken the
formula. Lose 10 points.

?38

A wash-out?
Lose 15 points.

Was there any proof she'd
killed him?

Yes **1**   No **2**

Did there appear to be any
motive for her killing
Morani?

Yes **3**   No **4**

Ans. **C** ....

STELLA ASKY

Could he have dragged the
chest from the river?

Yes **1**   No **2**

Could he have seen it
floating by?

Yes **3**   No **4**

Ans. **T** ....

TOM BELL

Was he the "minder"?

Yes **5**   No **6**

Was he the murderer?

Yes **7**   No **8**

Ans. **S** ....

HARRY COLLINS

Could she have been in it
together with Emily?

Yes **1**   No **2**

Did the lack of proof point to
her innocence?

Yes **3**   No **4**

Ans. **E** ....

ROSE BARKER

Was he the last to see
Plummer alive?

Yes **1**   No **2**

Did he appear capable of
overlooking important
details?

Yes **3**   No **4**

Ans. **M** ....

TODD BURGESS

Was his being left-handed
that significant?

Yes **5**   No **6**

Was there anything else that
could connect him with the
crime?

Yes **7**   No **8**

Ans. **A** ....

STEVEN CURTIS

Was he the "minder"?
Yes **1**   No **2**
Was he the murderer?
Yes **3**   No **4**
Ans. **S** ....

TOM BEAZLEY

Was there something in his
pocket to link him with the
crime?

Yes **1**   No **2**

Were the police wrong
about the significance of his
gloves?

Yes **3**   No **4**

Ans. **A** ....

GORDON CARROLL

Could he have placed May's
prints on the knife
afterwards?

Yes **1**   No **2**

Could he prove May lunged
at him?

Yes **3**   No **4**

Ans. **R** ....

CUTLER

55

Did he appear to be particularly observant?

Yes **1**   No **2**

Had it been fortunate he stood by the window to light his pipe?

Yes **3**   No **4**

Ans. **P** ....

MR. DALTON

Could she have been in it with Rose?

Yes **5**   No **6**

Did the lack of proof point to her innocence?

Yes **7**   No **8**

Ans. **E** ....

EMILY DOUGLAS

Was he the "minder"?

Yes **17**   No **18**

Was he the murderer?

Yes **19**   No **20**

Ans. **S** ....

CHICO GOLLANCZ

Did he have a motive for killing Gaston?

Yes **9**   No **10**

Could he be connected with the murder weapon?

Yes **11**   No **12**

Ans. **D** ....

BOB HARMON

Did she have a motive for killing Gaston?

Yes **1**   No **2**

Was she familiar with safety razors?

Yes **3**   No **4**

Ans. **D** ....

EMMA DEAN

Was he the "minder"?

Yes **13**   No **14**

Was he the murderer?

Yes **15**   No **16**

Ans. **S** ....

DICK FABER

Was there any motive for the killing?

Yes **5**   No **6**

Did he leave any evidence behind?

Yes **7**   No **8**

Ans. **P** ....

MR. X

Was it possible to play gin rummy all night?

Yes **1**   No **2**

Would she lie to protect her boyfriend?

Yes **3**   No **4**

Ans. **B** ....

GLORIA HARRIS

Was he the "minder"?

Yes **9**   No **10**

Was he the murderer?

Yes **11**   No **12**

Ans. **S** ....

DUTCH DEUTSCH

Was he as taken in by the ghost as he said?

Yes **1**   No **2**

Was there any proof his gun held blanks?

Yes **3**   No **4**

Ans. **G** ....

TOBY FRENCH

Did he have a motive for killing Gaston?

Yes **5**   No **6**

Could he be connected with the murder weapon?

Yes **7**   No **8**

Ans. **D** ....

BERT GREEN

Was there something peculiar about his victim's appearance?

Yes **5**   No **6**

Were there any visible signs of another auto?

Yes **7**   No **8**

Ans. **M** ....

HIT AND RUN DRIVER

Did he have a motive for killing Mrs. Pembroke?

Yes **1** No **2**

Could he have gotten in to murder her on the night in question?

Yes **3** No **4**

Ans. **I** ....

ALAN HOLLAND

Could he have lied about the previous attempt?

Yes **5** No **6**

Did he know more about the incident than he should have?

Yes **7** No **8**

Ans. **O** ....

THEO HUTCHINSON

Did she appear capable of killing Plummer for standing him up?

Yes **9** No **10**

Was there any motive for her killing Plummer?

Yes **11** No **12**

Ans. **M** ....

DESIREE MacINTYRE

Did the fact she lied prove her guilty?

Yes **1** No **2**

Was it likely she stabbed him without the taxi driver knowing?

Yes **3** No **4**

Ans. **Q** ....

POLLY MALONE

Was he likely to be on foot?

Yes **1** No **2**

Would he prove to be above suspicion?

Yes **3** No **4**

Ans. **H** ....

MR. X

Would she have let Tillie out of the box?

Yes **1** No **2**

Could she have made the snake bite?

Yes **3** No **4**

Ans. **N** ....

ISOBEL HUTTON

Was he in the best position to cover any loss?

Yes **1** No **2**

Was there any proof he had closer links with America than he admitted?

Yes **3** No **4**

Ans. **L** ....

JONATHAN MACKIE

Would he have fallen for Cutler's story?

Yes **5** No **6**

Did the facts fit?

Yes **7** No **8**

Ans. **R** ....

MAY

Did she seem suicidal?

Yes **1** No **2**

Was there anything peculiar about the shooting?

Yes **3** No **4**

Ans. **O** ....

DENISE HUTCHINSON

Was there something significant in his being "a separate traveller"?

Yes **9** No **10**

Was there something in his pockets linking him to the crime?

Yes **11** No **12**

Ans. **A** ....

DAVID JOINER

Was he the "minder"?

Yes **21** No **22**

Was he the murderer?

Yes **23** No **24**

Ans. **S** ....

"LUCKY" MacMILLAN

Was he too small-time a crook to be the murderer?

Yes **5** No **6**

Did his nickname give him an out?

Yes **7** No **8**

Ans. **H** ....

"LEFTY" MILLER

Was he the "minder"?

Yes **25**   No **26**

Was he the murderer?

Yes **27**   No **28**

Ans. **S** ....

FRED MITCHELL

Was the argument about the money important to her death?

Yes **5**   No **6**

Could the letter have been a forgery?

Yes **7**   No **8**

Ans. **I** ....

AGATHA PEMBROKE

Was it likely that in the attack he'd only wounded Barnabas once and sustained no wounds himself?

Yes **1**   No **2**

Would a pet normally turn on his master?

Yes **3**   No **4**

Ans. **F** ....

PHOEBUS

Did he have a motive for killing Gaston?

Yes **13**   No **14**

Could he be connected with the murder weapon?

Yes **15**   No **16**

Ans. **D** ....

ENRICO RAMPARDI

Was there any proof he'd killed himself?

Yes **5**   No **6**

Was it likely he was shot by someone hiding in the room?

Yes **7**   No **8**

Ans. **C** ....

TONY MORANI

Was it likely this was an outside job?

Yes **9**   No **10**

Could he know one of the men would dress as a ghost?

Yes **11**   No **12**

Ans. **G** ....

"MR. X"

Could she have disposed of the money before being stopped?

Yes **9**   No **10**

Was it apparent she was lying?

Yes **11**   No **12**

Ans. **C** ....

THELMA PORTER

Could his alibi be dangerous?

Yes **5**   No **6**

Could anyone have a full life without going to Hastings?

Yes **7**   No **8**

Ans. **B** ....

SHORTY REYNOLDS

Was it suspicious he was the last one down to breakfast?

Yes **13**   No **14**

Did something in his pockets link him to the crime?

Yes **15**   No **16**

Ans. **A** ....

JOHN PARKER

Was there some inconsistency in his testimony?

Yes **9**   No **10**

Did he have a motive?

Yes **11**   No **12**

Ans. **I** ....

GAVIN PEMBROKE

Was he as helpful as he sounded?

Yes **9**   No **10**

Did he have a vivid imagination?

Yes **11**   No **12**

Ans. **E** ....

RUPERT POSTLEWAITE

Was he particularly uncurious for a taxi driver?

Yes **5**   No **6**

Did he hurry back to the Station as fast as he could?

Yes **7**   No **8**

Ans. **Q** ....

FRED ROGERS

Was she able to use her position to best advantage?

Yes **5**   No **6**

Was America as distant a dream as she hinted?

Yes **7**   No **8**

Ans. **L** ....

EDNA SOMMERVILLE

Did he appear to be implicated in her death?

Yes **5**   No **6**

Did he have a motive for killing her?

Yes **7**   No **8**

Ans. **T** ....

PETER TARLTON

Did he have to pile books on the box?

Yes **9**   No **10**

Was he best placed to control Tillie's actions?

Yes **11**   No **12**

Ans. **N** ....

STANLEY TRILBY

Could he have shot him from the car?

Yes **9**   No **10**

Would he prove to be another small-time crook?

Yes **11**   No **12**

Ans. **H** ....

WELL-DRESSED FRIEND

Was there something peculiar about the blood on the secateurs?

Yes **5**   No **6**

Did the garden's appearance reflect the brother's work?

Yes **7**   No **8**

Ans. **F** ....

PETER TALGARTH

Could they have set Morham on this prank?

Yes **5**   No **6**

Could they have substituted live cartridges?

Yes **7**   No **8**

Ans. **G** ....

TWO FRIENDS

Did his story sound reasonable given the circumstances?

Yes **9**   No **10**

Was there any evidence to show he'd killed her?

Yes **11**   No **12**

Ans. **P** ....

MR. WARREN

Did she have a motive for killing Gaston?

Yes **17**   No **18**

Was it suspicious his having the safety razors?

Yes **19**   No **20**

Ans. **D** ....

TED WILSON

Was her "evidence" proof Shorty killed Baker?

Yes **9**   No **10**

Would she have known she'd be regarded as an accessory?

Yes **11**   No **12**

Ans. **B** ....

BARBARA TANNER

Might she be expected to bite more than once?

Yes **5**   No **6**

Was it easy for her to get out of the box?

Yes **7**   No **8**

Ans. **N** ....

TILLIE

Was he the "minder"?

Yes **29**   No **30**

Was he the murderer?

Yes **31**   No **32**

Ans. **S** ....

MANNY WEIDENFELD

Did his aggressive nature indicate his guilt?

Yes **9**   No **10**

Was there any real evidence connecting him to the thefts?

Yes **11**   No **12**

Ans. **L** ....

HENRY WOODHEAD

THE EVIDENCE

13

A You're not on the right trail. See clue 13 and lose 30 points.

B She's a card all right. But where's the evidence to suggest she was lying? Lose 20 points.

C You must be dumber than she is! See clue 35 and lose 30 points.

D She'll be sewing prison uniforms from now on. Award yourself 200 points for being sharp and read the Truth, p.63.

E Yes, there's proof that points to someone else. See clue 10 and lose 20 points.

F Your skill in deduction is going to the dogs. Lose 30 points.

G Your expression must be a blank one if you answered like this. See clue 18 and lose 20 points.

H "Above" is right, but not completely – try again and lose 10 points.

I There's a gap in your logic. See clue 5 and lose 30 points.

L You're way off course. Lose 30 points.

M Here's one occasion when it paid off to judge a book by its cover. Award yourself 150 points.

N Your answers are more hiss-terical than she is about snakes! See clue 3 and lose 30 points.

O You're not a very good judge of character. She wasn't that desperate. Lose 25 points.

P I don't think you have a clear view of the case. See clue 9 and lose 20 points.

Q You'd better get out and hitch – you're totally lost. Lose 30 points.

R No witness, no proof. Try again and lose 10 points.

S You're jumping to delusions – get a pen and paper and work it out. Lose 30 points.

T You're half right. Try again and lose 10 points.

14

A The compass probably sent you in the wrong direction. Study the case again and lose 25 points.

---

points.

C She was no genius, but she was no killer either. Lose 25 points.

D A jilted woman always has a motive. Lose 10 points.

E She wouldn't have the nerve to on her own, but you're right about her innocence. Try again and lose 25 points.

F You're half right, but you haven't collared the case yet. See clue 7 and lose 25 points.

G Look for proof and you'll draw a blank. Try again and lose 10 points.

H He was no sitting duck. Think again and lose 20 points.

I It wouldn't have been that easy since the door was locked. Lose 25 points.

L He probably doesn't even remember seeing the Statue of Liberty. Lose 25 points

M Your detecting is shoddy. Try again and lose 10 points.

N She's no Cleopatra. Try again and lose 25 points.

O Yes, you've answered correctly, so that should lead you elsewhere. Lose 20 points.

P It wasn't too fortunate for him! Try again and lose 10 points.

Q Taxi drivers must have good eyesight – why do you think he hadn't? Lose 25 points.

R You've obviously fallen for his story, but the wrong way. Try again and lose 20 points.

S He wouldn't hold a grudge for long. Think again and lose 25 points.

T Your detecting abilities are sinking fast! Lose 20 points and try again.

24

A Yes, he's not the man. Question another and lose 20 points.

B Serious card players are often oblivious to the time – anyway, what makes you doubt her statement? Lose 30 points.

C Yes, but it looks like you've questioned the wrong suspect. See clue 35 and lose 20 points.

D Your powers of observation and deduction need sharpening. See clue 31 and lose 20 points.

E Two heads usually are

---

better than one – why don't you ask someone to help you? See clue 23 and lose 30 points.

F So it's obvious that you're barking up the wrong tree. Lose 20 points.

G Good for you! You saw through his hazy testimony. But he probably wasn't the only one involved. Award yourself 75 points and investigate further.

H You're half right. See clue 14 and lose 10 points.

I You've got a blind spot. Try again and lose 20 points.

L Yes, it would be difficult for him to cover up. So question someone else. Lose 20 points.

M You're not addressing the problem. Try again and lose 20 points.

N You're right, so she's the wrong suspect. Try again and lose 20 points.

O You're not very perceptive for a detective. See clue 28 and lose 25 points.

P Unfortunately for him, maybe, but not for the police, who knew they had the right man. Award yourself 150 points.

Q Looks like you're in the wrong lane, doesn't it? See clue 27 and lose 20 points.

R You're on the knife's edge – try again and lose 10 points.

S You've gotten this far, so try again. Lose 20 points.

T He's stronger than he looks. Lose 10 points.

57

A You're only adding fuel to the fire. Lose 25 points and find a more likely suspect.

B Shorty seems to lead life to the full no matter where he goes, but what makes you think he's lying? Lose 20 points.

C Your answers contradict themselves. See clue 1 and lose 30 points.

D You're not very sharp today, are you? Lose 30 points and chance a clue.

E She's innocent, all right. See clue 10 and lose 20 points.

F Must be a slow mower. Lose 10 points.

G You haven't the ghost of a chance – try again and lose 30 points.

H You're right about "small-time" but what's in a name? Lose 25 points.

I Your answers point to her innocence. Lose 20 points.

L If you think you've answered correctly, dream on. You're only half right. Lose 10 points.

M You're seeing something that isn't there. Lose 25 points.

N She's not as strong as you think. Lose 25 points.

O Award yourself 100 points if you noticed his slip of the tongue.

P There's more to this case than meets the eye. See clue 9 and lose 30 points.

Q If his story is true, he must have been curb-crawling! See clue 27 and lose 10 points.

R You've taken a shot in the dark. Study the case again and lose 30 points.

S The chips are down, and so is your skill for deduction. Study the case again and lose 30 points.

T She hadn't seemed to have stood in his way at all – so what was the motive? Lose 25 points.

58

A Poor soul, whoever tried to set him up nearly did it. Lose 20 points.

B Yes, it is important to choose your friends carefully, but aren't you being a bit hasty about Hastings? See clue 8 and lose 25 points.

C Would a man who had wine, women and song (not to mention money) commit suicide? Try again and lose 25 points.

D What's his motive? See clue 31 and lose 25 points.

E Have you uncovered something else I should know about? See clue 23 and lose 25 points.

F The only gardening he'll be doing from now on is in the prison yard. Award yourself 100 points.

G An unlikely suspect. See clue 18 and lose 25 points.

H Small is right, so the suspect is wrong. Lose 20 points.

I A good detective mustn't be too emotional – or gullible! Study the case again and lose 25 points.

L Award yourself 150 points if you saw through her testimony.

23

A You're wrong – someone was trying to frame him. Lose 25 points.

B It's really none of your business what they did all night, but do you think she *had* to lie to protect him? See clue 8 and lose 25

B You're half right, but the answer isn't in the cards. See clue 8 and lose 25 points.

C Where's your proof? Lose 25 points.

D Sometimes a stitch needs to be undone. Lose 10 points.

E She might not be well paid, but does she look the sort to steal from a child? See clue 23 and lose 25 points.

F Your answers don't make sense. Lose 25 points.

G You've been taken in, too. Try again and lose 10 points.

H Yes, you've reached great heights in your detective work. Award yourself 100 points.

I He's not the type to go into a blind rage over the woman who jilted him. Anyway, do you think she really did? Lose 25 points.

L You've forgotten that he's only a junior – his work is checked thoroughly. Lose 25 points.

M This isn't a suitable answer. See clue 16 and lose 10 points.

N Her phobia was too great to let her get near the box. See clue 29 and lose 25 points.

O Do you really think she would do such a thing? See clue 4 and lose 30 points.

P He must have had eyes on top of his head! Try again and lose 10 points.

Q Where's any substantial evidence to implicate her? See clue 27 and lose 25 points.

R Award yourself 150 points for seeing through his lies.

S He wouldn't mind a man he hates. Think again and lose 25 points.

T Award yourself 150 points if you guessed his guilt.

M Address your questions to another suspect and lose 20 points.

N Right, so now question a Homo sapien. Lose 20 points.

O Are you a good listener? Study the case again and lose 10 points.

P You're wrong – no "mad killer" was involved here. See clue 9 and lose 25 points.

Q You're really going places now. Award yourself 100 points and read the Truth, p.62.

R You haven't grasped the gravity of the situation. See clue 32 and lose 25 points.

S You're no ace detective. Try again and lose 25 points.

T You should know by now that appearances don't mean everything. See clue 15 and lose 20 points.

67

A You need a formula to get you out of this one. See clue 37 and try again. Lose 30 points.

B The law tends to doubt the word of shady characters like Shorty, but is there any *real* evidence against him? Lose 25 points.

C The room was hardly big enough for any hiding places. See clue 35 and lose 25 points.

D No motive and no weapon, either. See clue 31 and lose 25 points.

E Whether or not they *might* have plotted, there's no evidence to prove her guilty. Lose 25 points.

F You'd better bone up on the case. See clue 24 and lose 20 points.

G Doesn't make sense, does it? See clue 18 and lose 25 points.

H You're a bit short on logic. See clue 14 and lose 30 points.

I The argument was petty, but a vital clue wasn't. Try again and lose 25 points.

L You must be dreaming. Lose 20 points.

M Have you had your eyes checked lately? See clue 16 and lose 30 points.

N Your answers haven't much bite to them. Think again, see a clue and lose 30 points.

O You're a bit naive. Try again and lose 10 points.

P You're missing some important clues. Study the case again and lose 25 points.

Q You've really been taken for a ride! But you're right to suspect him. Lose 20 points.

R Your facts are fiction. See clue 11 and lose 25 points.

S Don't bet on it. Think again and lose 25 points.

T Your logic is all afloat. See clue 38 and lose 30 points.

68

A You're half right, but you've got the wrong man. See clue 13 and lose 25 points.

B Hastings may have historical significance, but it's obvious that solving this case is a real battle for you. See clue 8 and lose 30 points.

C Your answers indicate you're questioning the wrong person. Lose 20 points.

D He's not the man you want, then. Try another and lose 20 points.

E You're probably the first to say "the butler (or in this case, the maid) did it." Lose 30 points.

F Where's the wound? Think again and lose 10 points.

G You've answered correctly, so you know he didn't do it. Lose 20 points.

H I don't think you really got the "low-down" on this case. See clue 14 and lose 25 points.

I You're blind to the facts. See clue 19 and lose 30 points.

L Aren't there advantages in being the boss's secretary? Lose 10 points.

M Peculiar or inappropriate? See clue 16 and lose 25 points.

N Never trust a snake. See clue 3 and lose 25 points.

O You're too trusting. See clue 4 and lose 20 points.

P Your answers point to someone else. Lose 20 points.

Q You're on the right track, just speed up your logic. See clue 27 and lose 10 points.

R You're leaning in the right direction, so you know he's not the man. Try again and lose 20 points.

S You may have called his bluff, but you haven't won – now try to find the right men. Lose 20 points.

T His story sounds pretty fishy to me. See clue 15 and lose 25 points.

911

A Give yourself a pat on the back and 200 points for solving this one.

B Wouldn't the sands of time have shown in the evidence? See clue 8 and lose 10 points.

C You've got her number, all right. Award yourself 150 points and read the Truth, p.63.

D He may have been a gay blade once, but he never used safety razors. Lose 25 points.

E If you call that helpful, I'm the man in the moon! Lose 10 points.

G Yes, they probably did set up the whole thing, but something else doesn't click. Award yourself 75 points and investigate further.

H You're looking at this case from the wrong angle. See clue 14 and lose 25 points.

I You've got an eye for the truth! Bringing despicable characters like Pembroke to justice makes a detective's job worthwhile. Award yourself 200 points.

L You're drowning in a sea of delusions. Lose 30 points.

M Like Miss MacIntyre, you're still wet behind the ears. Lose 30 points.

N Award yourself 200 points if you discovered the *real* snake in this case and read the Truth, p.63.

P What's your evidence? Study the case again and lose 25 points.

S If he saw these answers, you'd be pushing up tulips! Lose 30 points.

912

A You don't really think he's a keen birdwatcher, do you? See clue 37 and lose 10 points.

B Take a closer look at the evidence and lose 20 points.

C Her statements might put more light on the subject. Lose 10 points.

D Maybe his girl's heart was stolen by another, but

he hadn't the weapon to take revenge. Lose 20 points.

E Inspector Black wouldn't exactly be over the moon seeing answers like these. Study the case carefully and try again. Lose 20 points.

G They seem like a pretty explosive pair to me. Lose 10 points.

H You must be fond of tall tales. See clue 14 and lose 30 points.

I Wasn't another man's attention – and her real reaction – enough of a motive? Try again and lose 10 points.

L Maybe he just doesn't like cops. Lose 25 points.

M She must be a quick-change artist. See clue 20 and lose 25 points.

N You've overlooked a key fact. Study the case again and lose 10 points.

P Sounds like you've got the wrong man, then. See clue 9 and lose 20 points.

S You're wrong – he knew the minder was someone else. Lose 25 points.

1011

A Cars can be convenient, don't you think? Lose 10 points and try again.

B Ah, sweet revenge! Award yourself 100 points and read the Truth, p.63.

C I wouldn't put anything past her. Try again and lose 10 points.

D Jealousy may be enough of a motive, but what makes you think he used safety razors? See clue 31 and lose 30 points.

E Mama's pride and joy is not as clever as he thinks. Award yourself 200 points.

G Boys will be boys. Try again and lose 10 points.

H So you know he didn't do it. Lose 20 points.

I Return to the scene and lose 10 points.

L Have you seen something I haven't? Lose 25 points.

M What was her motive? Study the case again and lose 25 points.

N You haven't really unlocked the mystery yet. Lose 10 points and try again.

P The only thing that's unreasonable here is your answer. Lose 30 points.

S We're not speaking the

same language! Take notes and deduce the *real* murderer. Lose 25 points.

1012

A You must have suspected him for *some* reason. Try again and lose 20 points.

B She was well aware of her position, which was not beside her beloved, and that's all that mattered to her. Lose 10 points.

C Right suspect, wrong answers. Think again and lose 20 points.

D He'd have done anything to get his girlfriend back, but he didn't do this. Lose 25 points.

E The writing's on the wall – why can't you see it? Try again and lose 10 points.

G What are friends for? See clue 18 and lose 20 points.

H Whatever his reputation, he couldn't have done it. Lose 25 points.

I They say love is blind, but so is your guess. See clue 5 and lose 20 points.

L Then you must have the wrong man. Lose 20 points.

M Right, so question someone else. Lose 20 points.

N Some important facts have slithered through your fingers. Try again and lose 20 points.

P Reasonable or not, what evidence points against him? See clue 9 and lose 25 points.

S Yes, it's safe to go dutch with him. Study the information again and lose 20 points.

1315

A If you think there's evidence against him, you must be losing your marbles. See clue 13 and lose 30 points.

D He may have been edgy, but he only used straight razors. See clue 31 and lose 25 points.

S You must have a chip on your shoulder. Grab a pen and work it out on paper. Lose 30 points.

1316

A Somebody had to be last. There's nothing to implicate him. Try another and lose 25 points.

D His tongue may have been sharp, but he never used safety blades. Lose 20 points.

S You're not playing with a full deck. Try again and lose 25 points.

1415

A How could you suspect him – he's only a family man preoccupied by his children's hobbies. See clue 13 and lose 25 points.

D Your own barber must have taken too much off the top. Think again, chance a clue, and lose 30 points.

S Maybe the joker was wild, but he wasn't. Study the case again and lose 25 points.

1416

A You wanted to give him the axe, but he's not your man. See clue 37 and lose 20 points.

D Hatred may be motive enough, but he never used safety razors anyway. Lose 25 points.

S You've won this hand, but you weren't very lucky. Lose 20 points.

1719

D You're making some pretty cutting statements, incorrect ones too. See clue 22 and lose 30 points.

S Adios to your chances of promotion. Study the facts again and lose 30 points.

1720

D He may have been a temperamental artist, but he had no motive. See clue 31 and lose 25 points.

S He didn't mind at all. Work it out on paper and find out who did. Lose 25 points.

1819

D Not suspicious, really – they were the tools of his trade. Lose 25 points and try again.

S He may have been a hot-blooded gangster, but he didn't do it. Try again and lose 25 points.

1820

D He's not your man, though. Question someone else and lose 20 points.

S You're right, amigo. So question someone else. Lose 20 points.

2224

S Maybe you're lucky too – you've answered correctly. So now question someone else. Lose 20 points.

2123

S You must be down on your luck to answer like this. Try again and lose 30 points.

2124

S An unlucky guess. Study the facts again and lose 25 points.

2223

S Lucky for him that your second answer is wrong. Try again and lose 25 points.

2528

S You've been looking after the facts. Award yourself 75 points.

2627

S Has something slipped your mind? Lose 20 points.

2527

S He may have held a grudge, but he wasn't that sneaky. Lose 10 points.

2628

S You know who he *wasn't* – now find out who he *was*! Lose 10 points.

3031

S Jolly good show! It's porridge for him! Award yourself 75 points.

2932

S You're right to question him, but your answers are highly questionable. Lose 20 points.

2931

S He can't be both. Think again and lose 10 points.

3032

S There's something you're not mindful of. Try again and lose 10 points.

THE TRUTH

Q Inspector Black looked thoughtfully at Rogers as he was brought back for further questioning. "I don't know how you thought you could get away with it," said Black. You couldn't possibly have driven all the way out to Kew and back again with a dead man upright in the back seat – he would have toppled over almost as soon as you started moving."

J 50 points if you suspected as Black did that the pearls were stuck inside the water pipe. He knew that a water pipe never leaked twice at the same place once repaired; the metal is thicker at the join. He therefore suspected that the join wasn't what it appeared to be, and he was correct. Further investigation showed that Bond had earlier cut the pipe and used putty to fill the join, over which he had placed a coating of lead so it looked like a normal repair.

Black suspected that once they left, Bond would try to remove the pearls before the plumber came. "If he'd really been innocent," he said to Coombes, "why hadn't he called a plumber in earlier to fix the defective pipe? He obviously didn't because he had something to hide. . . ."

P Two things particularly bothered Inspector Black. Firstly, why stand out in the open to light a match in windy, rainy conditions – especially if there was a more sheltered place to do it? And secondly, he didn't think it possible for a shorter-than-average man to see the body from its position flush with the wainscotting from the front window in those conditions. In fact, he'd not been able to see the body from the window himself, and he was a fair bit (4 ins) taller than Mr. Dalton. Faced with these two significant slips, as well as excessive police curiosity as to the state of his collar, Dalton soon confessed to murdering Mrs. Warren. He'd made an appointment to meet her outside his office at 6.30 when he'd hoped to bring her back to his flat to see just how much she'd wanted her old job back. However, on the way there, she'd gotten cold feet and expressed a desire to go home to her husband, Dalton, however, became inflamed by her resistance. Realising they were quite close to a house he knew to be deserted, he suggested they wait out the worst of the storm in the doorway. Once there he continued his advances, which she resisted, and in pressing her against the door, it swung open and he dragged her inside. She put up a struggle, even leaving her fingerprints on his collar. Realising she was dead he finally collapsed – the shock proving too great. Thinking he'd use them as part of his alibi he'd called out to them with the story of how he'd seen the body when lighting his pipe – this stroke of imagination proved his undoing!

S By a process of elimination, Black deduced the following:
Beazley was not the "minder" (8) or the murderer (6);
Mitchell was not the murderer (6);
Deutsch was not the "minder" (7) or the murderer (9);
Weidenfeld was not the "minder" (7);
Collins was not the "minder" (8) or the murderer (10);
Faber was not the "minder" (8) or the murderer (10);
MacMillan was not the "minder" (9) or the murderer (9);
Chico Gollancz was not the "minder" (9) or the murderer (9).

Therefore, he knew that **Mitchell** was Charlie's "minder" and **Weidenfeld** his murderer!

T Peter Tarlton appeared to have the weaker story, but Black was too experienced to forget that appearances can be deceiving. Tom Bell definitely knew more than he was saying, but it was what he said that gave him away. It was impossible for him to have spied the trunk as it floated by. The amount of water penetrating the trunk would result in so decomposed a body, in the first place, that the trunk could never have floated. Tom Bell was arrested, therefore, as an accessory.

O While Inspector Black believed that Hutchinson probably didn't kill his wife himself, he was convinced, however, that Hutchinson knew who did. How else would he have known his wife had been shot? Black had heard every word the maid had said, and she hadn't mentioned what was wrong with Mrs. Hutchinson. Strange, then, that Hutchinson burst in saying "Who shot her?"

B Spending time in gaol was nothing to Shorty spending time in hell which was where Barbara wished him when she found out about Gloria. A mutual "friend" had spilled the beans recently about her being two-timed, hence the somewhat late confession – only it didn't wash. Black knew Shorty's gun couldn't have been buried all the time the case was unsolved – "With a girlfriend like that," thought Black, "Shorty didn't need any enemies!"

K 100 points if you guessed that Black headed south to find Little Zoë in the arms of her mother just about to board a flight to France. It was lucky for Black that Pettit's house was on a hill, as he couldn't have ascertained the direction on level ground. However, on a hill, all one has to note is which end of the studs have been pushed deeper in. If it's the front, or anterior end, the car is going downhill; if the back, or posterior end is deeper, the car is going uphill. This reflects where the weight is as the car advances, and so the direction.

C Black had to agree with Shakespeare that there's no fury like a woman scorned. Thelma was determined to show Morani that he should have thought twice about ditching her. But whether she really meant to kill him or just frighten him was what a jury would have to determine. It was enough for Black to know she'd shot him. "She should have come up with a better story," Black said to his constable. "There's no way she could have looked through the keyhole without seeing something if he had the light on."

D Constable Coombes agreed with Black that of the five suspects only three seemed to have had dealings with Gaston sufficient to provide motives — Rampardi, Hammon and Dean. Only two of the suspects familiar with the murder weapon — Wilson and Dean — seamstresses used safety razors to rip seams. Dean was the only one, therefore, with both a motive and a weapon.

Under questioning, Dean admitted using the blades on Gaston when he once again rejected her advances. When he remained cold to her, she inadvertently reached for the razor in her pocket and struck him with it.

L "Actually I really didn't have to interview them first," Black explained to Fakenham. "But I did want to see what sort of person I might be dealing with. I have to say she was cool as a cucumber." But criminals often go too far – like her helpful suggestions on who did it, etc. What clinched it, of course, was her application form – she'd written the date American style. No matter how much time you devote to learning another country's customs certain habits are so ingrained as to be practically eradicable."

F Inspector Black knew an inconsistency when he saw it. According to Peter, it usually took an hour for Barnabas to rake the leaves – yet in 45 minutes only a small portion had been done. Then, if Peter had really fought off Phoebus with the secateurs how come the hound was in such good shape? Nor did Barnabas appear to have a wound anywhere but on his neck.

"Poor Barnabus had a real friend in Phoebus," Black thought. He was positive he knew what happened. The dog's action points to the truth. He saw Peter attack the master he loved, and so he attacked the man he hated.

M Inspector Black felt there was something odd about this case. Primarily, what was a man well versed in male fashion doing in a light-coloured suit when he was about to go out with Miss MacIntyre? Proper attire would have been a dinner suit. He'd also been a little suspicious of the smashed watch and suspected it was a clumsy attempt by someone to fix the time of death. (In fact the medical examiner later said time of death had been around two hours earlier.)

I Like a lot of murderers, Mr. Pembroke tried to be just a little too clever! In describing the argument over his money, Mr. Pembroke indicated that there was a gap beneath the kitchen door large enough for a shilling to roll underneath. Yet, he claimed not to have smelt any gas until he entered the kitchen. Surely such a gap would have meant that the gas would have leaked up the stairs and into the adjoining rooms.

Convinced that the suicide note was a forgery, Black pretended to set it alight whereupon Pembroke forgot his blindness, and leaped for it. He'd only feigned his condition to get revenge on his wife for her feelings for Holland. The chloroform, which he claimed was to relieve pain suffered in frequent accidents caused by his blindness, was what he used to render his wife unconscious. Then it was easy for him to lay her in front of the oven.

R Black felt the whole story about the knife was a fabrication. Cutter could easily have inflicted that knife wound after he had shot May.

What really capped it for Black – that it was premeditated murder, was the fact that fragments of May's hat were found embedded in the skull wound. Had May sprung at Cutter and been shot he would have fallen forwards, not backwards. Black didn't doubt that Cutter had gotten May alone in the quarry on some pretext and had then cold-bloodedly murdered him before trying to make it look like self-defense.

A The British government was not the only one interested in Miller's formula. One of the four, Joiner, was a spy in the pay of a foreign power. He realized all along that he not only had to steal the formula but kill Miller. Otherwise, the scientist would have been able to duplicate his calculations.

Joiner made his plans carefully. Central to his plot was a carrier pigeon, which he brought down in his car, and carried in his pocket before stashing it in the wardrobe in his room, at Dr. Miller's. This bird had been specially trained to return to an accomplice at a selected place.

On the night of the murder, he crept downstairs after everyone was asleep, picked up Carroll's gloves from the hall, and went to the garage where he got out his jack and an axe. He also put on a pair of wellingtons that he found there. Using the jack, he prised open the bars on the laboratory window and walked to Miller's sleeping quarters, and stopped near the bed in a position in which a left-handed man would strike a blow. He quickly slipped out of his wellingtons, moved closer to the bed and killed Miller, who was still asleep. He found the formula and attached it to the neck of the pigeon which he set free. He then put the wellingtons back on and returned to the garage. He put the jack back in his car and the wellingtons in their place.

It was only extreme bad luck that the farmer, out hunting, shot down the bird and baffled by the papers round its neck, reported it to the police.

H Black knew right away that neither Lefty nor his companion had murdered Nugent, but he hoped they might lead him to the man that did.

It was obvious to Black, all along, that no one could have shot Nugent from the sedan, and have his bullet reach the 6-footer's neck and then travel downwards. It had to be someone outside the car!

E It was a long time before Rupert pulled another prank – he was confined to his room for weeks! But at least, Inspector Black told him, he could put the time to good advantage by studying the passage of the moon. As he would soon see, the moon in summer passes through the heavens in the south. It was impossible, therefore, for him to have seen a shadow on his wall, passing through moonlight coming from the hall window which faced north. The moonlight could only have come from the south-facing window in his room – the adjacent wall would have been dark!

G "Though I was convinced this was definitely murder," wrote Black in his report, "I wasn't certain whether French took advantage of the situation for his own purposes, or whether the others had been part of it as well.

French's testimony revealed he wasn't entirely innocent as he claimed the "ghost's" face was completely hidden. Yet the bullet hole, which penetrated the victim's forehead also pierced the sheet close to the bottom edge. Therefore, part of Morham's face would have been showing when he was shot.

N The key to the incident was – a key. Specifically, the key to Tillie's box. This was not in Devereaux's pocket where Black had expected to find it, but rather, upstairs in his bedroom. That meant to Black that someone else had opened Tillie's box, someone who was familiar with snakes and with Devereaux's house and habits. Black was convinced that Trilby was that someone. He and his assured handling of the snake convinced Black he could have managed the rest of the crime. "It's not all that difficult to extract a snake's venom and later inject someone with it. Since Devereaux didn't have his sleeping pills, I assume you drugged him with something else, most likely in his whiskey. I can't prove that, however, since only one glass is here. You'd have been wiser to remove both glasses – I felt one was rather suspicious. Once having drugged Devereaux it would have been a simple matter to inject him with the venom, unlock the snake, drink his milk and wish yourself good night."

Therefore, Inspector Black wasn't surprised at all that a search of Trilby's house turned up a small venom-collecting bottle and a double-needled syringe. He was only slightly surprised that evidence was uncovered which indicated that Trilby had been stealing money from the firm.

Master Record of Police Cadet

Cases investigated	Points earned	
The Riddle of the Sands		
Fare to Nowhere		
Man's Worst Friend		
The Covent Garden Mob		
Inside Job		
High Street Murder		
Marital Mishap		
Torch Song Tragedy		
A Winter's Tale		
Secrets of the Deep		
Quarrel at the Quarry		
Dressed to Kill		
Daring Death		
Repairing Fences		
Too Close a Shave		
The Taking of Little Zoë		
Deadly Hobby		
Pembroke's Poser		
A Problem of Security		
Ill Met by Moonlight		
Total score		

Great-uncle Henry's marking system became the basis for promotions throughout Scotland Yard. Compare your score with these ratings to locate your rank within the force. Should you have earned more than 3500 points, do not hesitate, but go directly to Scotland Yard and demand an office.

Scotland Yard Ratings:

0-500	Police Constable
500-1000	Sergeant
1000-1500	Inspector
1500-2000	Chief Inspector
2000-2500	Superintendent
2500-3000	Chief Superintendent
3000-3500	Commissioner